MW01709745

About Kyle

Life, Death and Beyond

A True Story

Angelina Petruso

PublishAmerica
Baltimore

First printing

ISBN: 1-4241-9110-6
PUBLISHED BY PUBLISHAMERICA, LLLP
www.publishamerica.com
Baltimore

Printed in the United States of America

This book is not only a story about my son Kyle.
It is a story about hardships, struggle, and loss.
It is a story about grief, recovery, and love.
It is a story about life, about strength, and about faith.

Author's Note

This book is a true story. I have orchestrated the events truthfully and completely as I have recalled them.

Although these events are true, the names of all the characters in this story have been changed to protect their identity—except for Kyle.

All events and circumstances that I have recalled in this book have been recollected from my memories and may not be in exact time line order or exact word-for-word re-enactments of Kyle's life. They are told in a way that evokes the real feeling and meaning of what I believe was said and my view of what actually happened.

Acknowledgments

I dedicate this book to my son, Kyle, who was loved and admired by many. His "unique" character was an inspiration to all who knew him.

It is also in memory of my father, Tony, and my mother, Nina, who tried so hard to love and nurture my sisters and me, even though their burdens were many. My father died of cancer at thirty-nine, and my mother struggled to raise her three girls alone.

I also could not have had the courage to write this book without the strength I found in my sister Giada, a cancer survivor, and the spiritual guidance my sister Tina gave me.

I must mention too, that the mentoring both Kyle and I received from my brother-in-law Leonardo made a positive effect on Kyle and made me the person I am today.

Contents

Chapter One

Beginnings

Sometimes, things happen when you least expect them, but for a reason. It is all in God's plan. On Friday, May 13th, my life was changed forever. Let me start at the beginning.

I was so disappointed when the obstetrician told me my baby was a boy. He was seven pounds, six ounces, and twenty-two inches long. Born on a very warm night in August of 1980, he was delivered naturally at 10:20 p.m. after seventeen hours of labor. His apgar score was good at nine. It was a Thursday, I believe. All along I had hoped for a little girl, but actually conceiving was going to be difficult for me.

I remember shopping with my sister at my favorite department store. Walking by the baby department made me burst into tears. I told her that my children would always be those little Scotty dogs that I was raising. That was my family. But after a minor surgery, I became pregnant the following month! I was going to be so happy, fulfilling one of my lifelong dreams. I always wanted to have a little girl that I could dress up in frilly little pink dresses with lots of ribbons and lace.

I couldn't believe that even with the ultrasounds I had, that the doctor could make such a mistake. First, she told me that I was going to have twins, and then with the next ultrasound, she only heard one heartbeat and told me it definitely was going to be a girl. Twins run in our family. My mother had a sister and brother that were twins.

Oh well, he was healthy and he had all his fingers and toes and he was mine. But when they put him in my arms and I gazed into his big blue eyes, something happened inside me. He looked right into my heart and I into his.

Joyfully, I said to him, "Hi, Kyle. I am your mother. You are my son."

The tears rolled down my face as I kept my eyes gazed upon his and held him firmly in my arms and gently rocked him. It didn't matter anymore that he wasn't a girl. I guess that is what they call bonding.

I was so ecstatic no matter what the sex of the baby. Kyle was really beautiful. I pressed my finger against his little chin as I talked to him and then I saw something in his mouth that made me gasp! He was born with a tooth! It was a little tooth right in front on his lower jaw. But it was loose. The doctor came in at that moment and told me he would have to put a string around it and pull it out, because he didn't want the baby to choke on it while he was nursing. Later that day, a nurse came in with the tooth wrapped in a little plastic cup for me to save as a memento of his birth. From this beginning, I knew he was going to be different and I would hear the word "unique" referred about him many, many times over.

After a couple of days in the hospital, I couldn't wait to go home. Packing all my belongings and flowers for the trip home that morning made me happy and excited. I couldn't wait to leave the hospital with my newborn son. But I quickly developed the patience of Job while I waited for the nurse to push me in the wheelchair to the elevator. When I finally made it into the car with the baby, I was so excited to get him home. The drive to the country seemed so long, but when we approached the driveway, I was told about the thunderstorm the other night and that the windows were left open to air out the house.

I didn't realize just how much of a mess that thunderstorm made. When I stood in the doorway, I was overwhelmed and started to cry. The storm wreaked havoc on the house. Not only were the windows left open, but the dogs were not secured in the basement kennel. The front door was left open but the screen door was locked. The screen kept the dogs in, but it didn't keep the rain out. I guess the thought was that the storm would freshen up the air inside, but I came home to a disaster! All the curtains were soaked and stained as well as the windowsills. The carpet at the front door was soaked with rainwater. The four Scotty dogs ran free through the house and unrolled toilet tissue from one end of the house to the other. One of the Scotties was so nerved up from the storm that he chewed the carved wooden arm and the upholstery of my new Victorian-style chair by the living room window. It was ruined! The basement had two inches of water in it and both the washer and the dryer were damaged and needed repair before I could do any laundry.

On top of a!! of this, I was expected to clean everything up by myself and couldn't get any help from my family at all—especially not from my mother. I was told that I would still be expected to have meals at the table on time. The house was to be kept in order at all times and I couldn't even think about lying down to rest. That would be unacceptable!

The house and family life was not going to change just because of a baby. I guess I was in a little shock from what I heard and from what I saw there at the house. I spent so much time decorating it and making it into a beautiful home. But even though I was full of stitches and still weak from the labor and delivery, I put the baby down in his bassinet and began cleaning up the mess. That was when reality set in. I knew then that my life had changed, but not with the happiness of bringing home a new baby. It was like a dark cloud settled over the roof from that thunderstorm and it was not going to dissipate with the wind. Eventually, I would have to make a decision about raising my son. It would be a decision that would take me about three years to get up enough courage to make.

After a couple of weeks, Kyle was finally getting on a schedule that I could handle, since I was the only one getting up with him in the middle of the night. At Kyle's first checkup after his birth, his doctor noticed another strange thing. Kyle's breastplate was underdeveloped. The doctor thought that Kyle might have to undergo surgery to invert it if it didn't grow properly. It was sunken in and very thin. Every breath he took made his little breastplate sink in and out. I would have to be very careful when handling him. I would have to decide on an operation if it didn't improve by the next office visit. I was so scared for his life. I prayed constantly to God and by the one-month checkup, it had improved. I thanked Him for answering my prayers. Now hopefully, things would all settle down and I could breathe easily.

I did all the cleaning and laundry during the day while I was alone. I was able to handle my duties within the house and as a new mother because I was determined not to cause any friction. I kept telling myself that just because there was a new baby in the home, life shouldn't be any different. Before this, I thought that raising a family would be an easy task, being in my early thirties and much more mature. I felt that things wouldn't be as much of a struggle. The house was already secured and decorated in style. There was no fear of financial problems. I still had my teaching position and would return to it after my six-week maternity leave. But the school had its own problems with finance and the funds that were raised to keep it running were just not enough. The school was scheduled for closing after the next term. I thought that I probably would have to start looking for a new teaching position before the next school year would start, but I couldn't worry about that right now. I had enough to worry about with the baby.

I didn't think that I would become pregnant again so soon though. I guess I didn't even think about protection like I should have. I was obedient because I didn't want to do anything to rock the boat. So I gave in, even though I still had internal stitches and sex was painful to me. But then I was truly glad when I became pregnant again. Maybe another child would help the relationship. Maybe I would feel loved if I could have a little girl. Maybe that was what it would take, so I prayed for a little girl again.

My wish came true when my little Katerina was born only a year and two days after Kyle! I had another natural delivery with only twelve hours of labor and no complications. She was so beautiful with those chubby little cheeks and thick black, curly hair. I felt that she was truly a blessing. Life was going to be great now.

I thought I could handle two little ones by myself, but I found out differently very soon. Katerina was a very excitable and a nervous little baby. I guess it is true what they say about a baby feeling emotions from within the womb. I know that even though I tried to handle my emotions, deep down inside I was always nervous and unhappy with my marriage. I know this was the message I must have been sending her. She was drinking about one ounce of milk every hour and spitting most of it up after each feeding. She had an underdeveloped esophagus and stomach; and she had difficulty keeping her food down. It must have been because she was three weeks premature.

After a couple of months of struggling with her and trying to give both of them the attention they demanded, I was a frazzled mess with no help or support. Everything was falling apart but I didn't want to accept it yet. Eventually, after another year or so, I would see this happening. But for now, I had my hands full. I just kept hoping that things would change for the better.

Thank God, Kyle was such a good infant. He was easy to keep on a schedule when he was a new baby. When he was little like Katerina, I had him eating every four hours and he kept quiet in his crib or playpen. I could even go downstairs to put a load of laundry in and when I came up, everything would still be fine with Kyle. But Katerina was a different story. She demanded much more attention. Now with the two of them, I could hardly keep up with everything. When she started crawling and Kyle toddling around, I couldn't leave them for a minute. One time I found her climbing up in the rocking chair and trying to stand up in it! She wasn't afraid of anything.

I think the reason that Kyle was more cautious was because of the accident he had when he was about six months old and walking in the walker. I was pregnant with Katerina at the time. He was speeding through the kitchen in the walker and rammed right into the screen door. I never thought to lock the screen. I should have locked it because we were working on a new room off the kitchen. It was on a lower level and the stairs were not in place yet. When Kyle rammed into the screen, the door opened and he fell about four feet, head down, into a pile of sand! All I could do was stand there at the door and scream for someone to come and get him. Being pregnant, I couldn't jump down over him without possibly falling right on him. He wasn't moving at all and I thought he had died. My screams for help were heard and quickly Kyle was picked up off of the sand pile and pulled out of the walker. Kyle's face was covered in sand and I think he had knocked the wind out of himself. After the sand was cleaned out of his mouth with the garden hose, he finally started screaming. I was so relieved to hear him cry. At the emergency room, I was told that he was just going to have a lot of bruises—nothing broken, and just a slight concussion. I thanked God over and over that he was okay.

The next visit to the emergency room was for Katerina. When she was six months old, she developed a terrible middle ear infection that required a stay in the hospital. With antibiotics and the excellent care she received at the hospital though; she was able to go home after a couple of days. I stayed with her though—day and night. But when Kyle was around eighteen months old, he developed a high fever with an ear infection. It was a different story for him. I was alarmed, but not to the extent that I should have been. All babies go through fevers and most get ear infections at times, I thought, and I had already been through this with Katerina. But he was older than Katerina when this happened to him. Again in the middle of the night, he was taken to the emergency room. This time the doctors had to flush his ears out with water. It was a very painful procedure but it had to be done. The attending physician noticed that there was a hard kernel of corn in one ear and a dried pea in the other! Yes, he was finding places other than his mouth to put his food! It was only a few weeks after that episode that I realized why he was holding his food in his cheek and not eating well anymore.

My niece Rochelle, who is a nurse, noticed that his tonsils were infected. They were so swollen and infected that he was really hurting when he tried to swallow. So he was back at the hospital again, and this time for an emergency tonsillectomy.

Because of the procedures and testing they have to do for operations, the doctors found something even more serious than his tonsils. I was told that he was a severe diabetic! My whole world was falling apart. With Katerina demanding so much of my attention, I neglected to really see what was happening to Kyle. He was close to being two years old and now this serious disease! I was told that if he didn't start on insulin shots, I would lose him forever. His sugar was over 400! I tried to understand why these things were happening to my family. I tried to keep on going and not show my worries, but it was easy for anyone to see through my façade.

Nevertheless, I knew that something must be done for him so I sought the help of a new pediatrician on the hospital staff. He was a specialist in pediatric diabetes. I felt that since my niece worked with him, she would know the best doctor for my little boy. He gave Kyle one milligram of insulin to see if it would trigger his pancreas to start functioning properly. Thankfully, after the tonsillectomy and extensive consultation with the doctor, Kyle's sugar maintained normal levels and he was able to go home. For six weeks I monitored his blood sugar levels three times a day and kept him on a strict diet. At the same time, I was trying to devote the same attention to my little girl, who still seemed nervous and excitable. It was quite a struggle for me. I prayed a great deal and worried a bit; but with the support and prayers from my family and Kyle's new doctor, his blood sugar stayed within normal ranges every day. Katerina was also calming down now and becoming a happy baby. Through all of this though, I felt like I was the only person caring for both of them. There was no help at all unless there was company over. Then a good show would be put on, with people around, and great care was shown for the two of them. Diapers would even be changed in front of the company, just for show, but as soon as they would leave, things would go right back to normal.

My daily routine of cleaning and cooking and caring for the children kept me busy, but I still had to find a way to get some spending money, since I wasn't working. I wanted to be able to buy clothes for the kids as they grew out of the ones they had, and other things that they needed. When I could gather enough items together, I would have a garage sale to get some money so that I could buy clothes and play things for them. I also figured that if I mowed the lawn while the kids were taking a nap, I would be given a little money for the job. This worked for a while, but when I wanted to take the extra car and go shopping with the kids, I would find that the distributor cap was missing so I couldn't start the car! I was getting the feeling that I was being kept as a slave and a workhorse or something! I did need to get out once in a while, or I would explode! That is why I called my mother or my sister or nieces to pick us up and take us places when I needed to get out. Things were made difficult for me, but I still found a way. I remember one time my nieces took us shopping and then out to lunch. It was a fun day for the kids because they got to go to their favorite fast food restaurant. I was happy too, because I still had enough money left over for milk. I guess that day really made an impression on my nieces. They realized how difficult life was becoming for me.

When the children's first and second birthdays were approaching, I had a small family party for them at home. My family showered them with all kinds of clothes and toys. My mother bought Kyle his new little shoes and my sister Giada bought him the cutest little pair of yellow oil overalls with short pants. A railroad cap from Kyle's grandfather was made over to fit him, and we bought him a little train. It was so cute watching him sit on it and chug-chug around the house with it, tooting the whistle. But when he realized we were looking at him and laughing, he started to really cry. He thought we were teasing him. He was so sensitive.

Since Katerina was just a year old, she didn't really understand most of the party—except for the cake and ice cream. She really loved to eat. She received many toys and clothes but she especially loved her little pink blanket that I made her. She carried that around with her for many, many years.

Eventually, I was able to enjoy a little time to myself once in a while, to work on a few crafts. I loved to crochet and sew and refinish furniture, when I had the time. Working on crafts was relaxing for me. I tried to save money by making my own curtains or making the kids a few clothes, or even quilting a blanket for them.

I enjoyed going to auctions once in a while because I loved antiques, so if there was something there that was repairable, it was purchased. Then I would refinish the wood and the necessary hardware was repaired. We found this really old antique baby buggy at one of the auctions. It looked just like a pile of scraps, until it was put back together. I reworked some of the wicker cane decorations on the sides of the buggy, and refinished the wooden seat. My sister Giada re-upholstered the seat cushion and covered the parasol in the prettiest yellow brocade fabric to match. I also sewed some gold fringe on the parasol, which made it look adorable. We really enjoyed taking the kids to the fair in this buggy—especially on senior citizen's day. The older folks stopped us every few feet to tell us their story about times past—when they had a buggy like that. It made the fair a very enjoyable time for all of us.

Kyle & Katerina in the stroller at the county fair

Even though there were some great times, troubles were brewing to a rolling boil. There was a period of about six weeks that the communication came to a halt. But that was after I landed in the hospital.

I think back in disbelief at what I went through with my poisoned liver and those ten days that I spent in the hospital. I just couldn't believe that I was deliberately poisoned, but that was what the doctors told me when the lab report showed evidence of toxins in my blood!

I still kept hoping that things would get better as the children grew, but eventually something had to be done. Scheduled appointments with a psychologist were arranged. But seeing a psychologist for counseling didn't seem to help at all. I let it all out and told him everything that was upsetting me. But the blame was all put upon my actions and behavior. After that, things were still the same, but I really thought there would be hope.

Since this doctor was in another city, I asked my sister to come along with me once so that the two of us could go shopping after my visit. My mother was watching the kids at the time, so I felt I could spend a little time shopping in the area afterward. When we arrived at the appointment, my sister asked me if I wanted her to come in with me. I thought that was kind of odd, so I told her I didn't need her in there with me. Why would she want to come in with me anyway? I didn't need any help telling my side of the story. I was capable of going in alone. She didn't say anything more at the time, so the subject was dropped. During that visit though, the psychologist asked me if I wanted any medication and if I would check into the hospital for a few weeks to rest. I couldn't understand what he was trying to tell me. There was no way that I could do that! I didn't need any medication! My liver was already poisoned enough! I didn't need a stint in the psych ward! How could he ask me to do such a thing! I bluntly told him no and the subject was dropped.

When I got back into the car, my sister asked me how it went. I told her what he asked me to do and how confused I was about it all. She didn't really have any comments to say and that was confusing to me also. It was later in the week that I found out why. My sister told me later that she had secretly called the doctor that week; after she had a strange visit. She listened to the complaints about me like she always did. She was told that there were phone calls placed to the doctor after our sessions, and things were told to him that I supposedly did. These things were said to make me look like I was crazy. My sister just listened, and didn't give any rebuttal. She was a good listener. But there was one big mistake made this time. While my sister was listening to all of the problems with me, some subconscious thoughts slipped out. While thinking out loud at one point, she heard that the plan was to convince the doctor that he should declare me insane! The psychologist could actually put me in the psych ward and have the kids taken away from me! This plan was perfect in thought. The only problem was that my sister also had a plan. She secretly called the doctor herself and let him know what was really going on. She told him what was said to her and how I was going to be railroaded into the insane asylum. Finally, this plan backfired and the doctor realized who actually needed help! The only trouble was that a person with this type of personality disorder usually denies that they have a problem, and never gets any help. So we were back at square one. I had to either live with someone that didn't love me, or leave. That was just too much for me to deal with at the time, so I let it go.

During that summer, my niece Marie was getting married and Kyle and Katerina would be in the wedding as the ring bearer and flower girl. I made Kyle a little black tuxedo jacket with silk lapels and short pants. It somewhat resembled the groom's tuxedo. I also made the little heart-shaped pillow for him to carry the rings on down the aisle. I made Katerina a little floor-length dress just like all the dresses the bridesmaids wore. It was easy for me to copy the style of clothing, even without any pattern.

As the wedding day approached, they both were excited to be in it. I was nervous for them. They both were so young that they really didn't understand exactly what they were expected to do during the ceremony. I remember Katerina having a hard time carrying the basket of flower petals. It was almost as big as she was at the time! She did it though, with just a few stops on the way up the aisle to scatter the petals. She was really cute to watch and everyone chuckled when she sat down a few times in the middle of the aisle! Eventually, she made it up to the front of the church. Next was Kyle's turn. He was coaxed a little with a gentle push, but he became overwhelmed when he saw everybody staring at him and quietly laughing. He started crying and screaming so much, that he had to be guided up the aisle by one of the bridesmaids. My sister and brother-in-law kept him next to them to calm him down. It was quite a memorable moment during the ceremony when the photographer captured him in a full scream in front of the wedding party! It was a moment that he would never live down.

Kyle & Katerina in my niece's wedding

Later on at the reception, I had an embarrassing moment myself. I always loved to dance, but I couldn't coax anyone out on the dance floor. I knew that I couldn't get out on the dance floor alone, so I begged and pleaded for someone to go out on the floor and dance with me. After a few drinks, I was glad that there finally was an agreement. It was a fast dance and we could dance any way we wanted to and not be noticed. We began to dance, but before I realized what was happening, I was grabbed close against him. Instead of hugging me, the skirt of my dress was pulled way up, exposing my undergarments to everyone! I kept trying to push my skirt down, but I could hardly get my arms out from under his grip. When I finally broke loose, I ran outside crying of embarrassment. I heard the tremendous laughter while I was escaping, about the great joke that was played on me. There was no sympathy for my feelings or how horrible that incident was for me. I finally was able to get my composure and went back into the reception, but all I heard was how fat I had become after having two children. It was things like that episode that helped to push me over the edge.

In that same summer month, when the children were approaching their third and fourth birthdays, I thought I would try to give them a nice party. I had a good friend that had been married for many years but never had any children of her own. Denise and her husband Tim made up for it in other ways. Denise had designed a costume for her husband to wear that resembled the big yellow bird on the children's television show. She was so creative that she even sewed little yellow feathers all over it and designed the feet and wings and beak just like the television character. Tim was a tall man and he looked great in the bird costume. They would get a lot of happiness out of walking in the parades in our area and talking to the little children that came up to see him dressed like the yellow bird. I think it made their lives less lonely for a child of their own.

I thought that I could give our two children a great birthday party with the yellow bird there to meet and greet the kids. It would be a very special day for them. I sent out about twenty-five invitations and ordered a special cake that was decorated like the yellow bird. I also bought all the party decorations and favors in the yellow bird theme. We even rented a tent and put it up in the back yard for the party. Since this was in August, it would most likely be fair weather, but the tent would keep the sunshine and maybe the rain off of the little ones. The children and I, along with my sister's family, were getting real excited as the day of the party approached.

The day turned out beautiful weather-wise, but the party was ruined. Our yellow bird friend was ready and waiting for all the little guests to show up. We were all waiting too—almost all of us. We waited and waited but the only one to show up for the party was my niece's little boy. I felt pretty bad for my children. They were so excited to show off their yellow bird friend to all their little companions, and none of them came to the party. We waited for over an hour, and then I thought about calling them. Maybe some of them didn't receive their invitations or maybe some of them had other commitments? I couldn't understand why all those children I invited didn't show up! After a few phone calls though, I found out why. Everyone that I called told me that someone called them and told them that the party was cancelled! What a mean thing to do! It was bad enough to hurt me, but to do this to the children was a different story. This incident almost pushed me over the edge. But it was the next confrontation that really did it for me.

Kyle & Katerina at their Yellow Bird Birthday Party

That day, I just came back from the oral surgeon, because I had a tooth removed. My mouth was pretty sore and the left side of my face was swollen. There was an argument over the placement of a few fruit trees in the back yard, but that was just the trigger for the real argument to begin. I realize now that there shouldn't have been any confrontations in front of the kids, but there were. I guess Kyle was too attentive at those times and really sensed the problems growing. While we were outside arguing about the trees, Kyle decided to play in a sand pile and started putting some into the open gas tank of the lawn tractor. I felt so bad for Kyle because I knew that he would be punished severely when the sand in the gas tank was discovered, but I was not going to say anything about it. Then while the argument continued inside the garage, Kyle came in and started playing with a wrench while listening to the conversation. When he was discovered and told to get out of the garage, he ran screaming at the top of his lungs and got into the back seat of my car in the driveway. That was when I noticed the distraught look on his face. He wasn't screaming because he was scolded, he was screaming because he was ready for a nervous breakdown. I'll never forget that look on his face. He needed to get away from all the anger and go somewhere where he could calm down and feel at peace. I had to do something. My heart hurt badly for my child and I realized I had to do something to help him. That is when I finally made my decision to leave.

Chapter Two

New Surroundings

I contemplated leaving soon, so I set a few personal items aside for the kids and myself, and hid them from view. So when the truck was gone, I grabbed what I had already packed and put the items in my car. I also filled a grocery sack with some toys for the kids, and I got some things from the basement for the dogs. I knew that there was no way that I could take all the four adult dogs and the seven puppies with me, so I just took the puppies and their mother. At least that way I could sell the puppies when they were ready, and have some money to live on for now. At the time, a Scottish terrier puppy would each bring in at least $350. I finally gave up and threw in the towel, so we all piled into my little car, and took off for my mother's house in town. It was then that I made the decision to start divorce proceedings.

I contacted my family's lawyer and he agreed to see me. Both of my sisters used to baby-sit for him when his children were young, so he knew of me. He was an old-time lawyer who was well respected in our community and was not afraid to take on this divorce—even though we both knew it would be a nasty fight over the children.

At the first court hearing, the judge ordered us to sit down with our lawyers together in the back room of the court, and discuss property divisions. There were so many personal property items, that it took us all day to divide everything up. There were even disagreements over the placements of the dogs! I knew that some items would be very hard to give up, especially things that could be cherished for their memories. I was able to claim most of the items that were mine beforehand. Most of those items were actually given to me by my mother, or they were things that I had acquired after my father's death for keepsakes. Pictures that he painted, and some of his belongings, were all that I had to remember my father by, since he died when I was an infant.

When we finally came to a decision, it was ordered that I would be able to go back to the house to pick up my property. I knew there would be a lot of furnishings and clothes, and things for the kids, so I got several of my friends together to help me move them to my mother's house. I should have had a police escort with me also, because when my family and friends arrived there with me, everything was scattered all over the front lawn! It must have been there overnight, because the paper sacks filled with clothes and things were all wet from the early morning dew. Most of the bags fell apart when we tried to pick them up. That was bad enough, but when I found the oil paintings that my father made, thrown on the lawn, I broke down in tears. I guess I was lucky that everything was still there, being left out overnight. Someone could have stopped there and taken everything in the night before we arrived! This incident was just the start of many occasions that would drag this divorce on for a period of over seven years.

My family decided to let me rent my grandparents' house temporarily, but I needed to fix it up first before we could move in. There were several renters in the past that practically destroyed the place. But this would be an easy move for me since I practically grew up in that house. While my mother was working, I spent time with my grandparents there as a child. I felt safe there and I would try to make the children feel safe there as well. We would call it our happy house. This house would bring back a lot of good memories for me from my childhood. I especially remember smelling the loaves of homemade Italian bread baking in the oven. My grandmother made seven loaves of bread every week, but she always made me a special little loaf when she knew I was coming over to visit. She would break it open hot, right out of the oven, and put salt and pepper and the best olive oil on it. It was so delicious!

Sometimes, my mother would drop me off at my grandparents' house before she went to work. I would get there just in time for breakfast. It was a real treat because we always had a special kind of cereal. It was an Italian peasant breakfast of day-old bread, broken up in a bowl, with milk, sugar, butter, and a splash of cappuccino on it. I remember them calling it pane latte.

Before I could move in though, my sister Giada and my cousin Donita agreed to help me fix up the place. It had sat empty for several months because of the needed repairs. The kids and I stayed with my mother, temporarily, so we could get the work done on the house. It was very hard though, for my mother. She wasn't in the best of health, and having to deal with the children didn't help at all. Kyle was especially difficult back then. Being a year older than Katerina, he was much more aware of what was happening. He just couldn't understand why he was told to get out of the house. He was angry and confused and I know the poor little kid felt like he caused all of the turmoil. For the longest time, he felt that everything was all his fault. To show his anger, he lashed out at Katerina and at my mother. At times, my mother just couldn't keep up with him. The two of them fighting and screaming was enough to bear, but at one point, Kyle even tried to set my mother's living room curtains on fire! Even though she tried to keep them busy, there were times when she found them scribbling with crayons all over her kitchen walls or ripping up photos. Kyle would especially love to bang on the piano or fight with Katerina over some toy that he didn't want to share with her. He was really being difficult, but we knew why, and we tried to understand and comfort him and Katerina.

But this move would be a fresh start for us. It was a nice three-bedroom home in the city and the best elementary school was just a couple of blocks away. A new beginning in a new place might calm the children down somewhat so that we could have peace and harmony again in our lives.

There was a tremendous amount of work to be done. There were broken windows and a cracked water heater, as well as damage to the wrought-iron porch railings and broken cement steps. The hardwood floors were gouged, scratched, and very dirty. There also were missing tiles in the kitchen walls. On top of all of that, the chimney had to be partially taken down and rebuilt because of cracks in the mortar and broken bricks. The building inspector tagged it because it could have caused a gas leak and the whole place would have exploded if it were not repaired. Of course, all the rooms had to be cleaned and painted. The old carpeting had to be taken out and all the hardwood floors had to be cleaned. I was going to remove the carpeting and use throw rugs for now. There was grease so thick on the kitchen cupboards though, that I could scrape it off with a putty knife! I thought that was bad enough, but the house had to be exterminated several times to rid the place of roaches! It took several months to accomplish all of this. During that time, my poor mother was trying to deal with my two angry little children.

When I was finally able to bring the children into the house, it was empty but very clean and freshly painted. The thought of the freshly painted empty rooms makes me remember the first thing that Kyle did when I showed him his bedroom. He was so excited that he ran directly to the old iron hot water heater and turned the nozzle on. The water streamed all over the floor! Before I could turn the water off on his heater, he ran into Katerina's room and did the same thing! He was very quick and I knew I would have my hands full to keep him out of trouble. He was so excited about the new house that he ran back down the steps, out the front door, and into the street! I screamed for him to get out of the street as I ran after him. Since we lived in the country thus far, he was never in a city yard where the streets were paved and the sidewalks were close to the houses. I was frantic! What if a car would have been driving by and hit him! I scooped him up and ran back into the front yard and I scolded him and warned him never to go into the street again. I had a flashback of when I was nine and drove my bicycle into the street without looking and was almost hit. I knew now that I would have to watch both of them very closely, especially in the front yard.

As moving-in day approached, there was more than just furniture that brought us excitement. As my cousin Donita was shaking out the sheets to make up Katerina's mattress on the floor, a rather large roach crawled out between the folds of the crisp white sheets! I just stood there and screamed. I'll never forget Donita's bravery though, and quick wit. She was able to snatch the creature right up in her hand and quickly flush it down the toilet! This meant that I would have to call the exterminator back for another round of visits to get rid of those nasty creatures.

At the time, we didn't have much furniture to move in with. All that we had was borrowed from my family. My brother-in-law Leonardo was kind enough to buy us a television for the living room. At least we would still be able to enjoy our favorite programs. The kids' rooms had mattresses on the floor at first, until I could find them some bed frames. My sister Giada and my cousin Donita had helped me paint earlier, and now they helped me move in the furniture. My sister gave me a couple of end tables and lamps, and a couch. My mother gave me an upholstered chair for the living room, and a kitchen table and chairs. I was thankful that my family pitched in and supplied me with all the rest of the necessities to complete the kitchen and bathrooms. I was also able to locate bed frames and dressers for our clothes the next week. I found a cute little child's table and two chairs for the kids at a garage sale. It was nice to have it in the living room by the television so they could draw and do crafts as they watched their favorite shows. After a few weeks, it was finally becoming a home instead of just a house. But again, Kyle tried to set the curtains on fire at our new little house! I knew he was still angry over the divorce, so I tried not to scold him.

During this period of adjustment, there were a few accomplishments along with a few setbacks.

They always say, "Two steps forward, and one step back."

I avoided looking for a job temporarily because I knew that the children would need me at home with them for now. We all needed to heal emotionally from the separation. Since my mother relinquished my piano, I felt that I could at least give piano lessons to some of the children in the neighborhood. The private school where I taught before Kyle was born closed down, so I would have to look for a new teaching position in the next year, hopefully at one of the parochial schools in town. But now I needed to concentrate on my own children.

I made a few phone calls, and got appointments for the three us to see a psychologist through Social Services. Counseling would help all of us get through this, but Kyle seemed to need a little more help.

After a few months, Kyle's psychologist felt that he needed more counseling, and not just help in dealing with the divorce. I was told that Kyle was regressing more and more into the fantasy world for comfort. He sought protection from his fears through the super heroes he most admired. He started obsessing over Superman and Inspector Gadget and then Mr. Banks from *Mary Poppins*, for comfort. I didn't mind when he wanted to wear his Superman pajamas or the red cape all day. It was okay that he had to carry his Inspector Gadget doll around with him everywhere, but I knew he was drifting further and further away when he insisted on wearing his Santa Claus hat in the middle of the summer!

One time when my sister Giada was watching him, Kyle begged her to let him wear a pair of her panty hose so that he could be Robin Hood. He told her they were "panty toes" and not panty hose. She thought that was smart of him, so she let him wear them while she took him shopping. This was Kyle's way of dealing with the mental and physical abuse that the psychologist reported to me. Kyle became very close to his counselor. Katerina was also opening up to her psychologist as well. The drawings that she made led her counselor to believe that something more was going on with her, besides her anger over the divorce.

I knew that Kyle had been treated unfairly at times, but I didn't realize how much of an effect it had on him. Kyle seemed to thrive on negative attention; and he would do things just to see how far he could push someone before they would react. It seemed that Kyle was playing mind games and that he knew just exactly how to press a person's buttons.

I found out eventually through the psychologist though, that Kyle's emotional problems were the result from a much more deep-seated problem than what I was aware of. I also heard from Katerina's psychologist that she was also showing signs of emotional difficulties of some kind. She was drawing lots of pictures of the same thing. We all asked her what she was drawing but she wouldn't really say anything. We thought that the pictures looked like big purple ghosts, but we found out later that they were implying something of a more disturbing nature. I also felt that something wasn't right with her because she was so angry most of the time. I hoped and prayed that all of this would eventually come out through their counseling.

As weeks went by, I felt that this whole thing was becoming a nightmare. Something was happening when the children were not in my care, but I couldn't explain any of it because they were very closed mouth about it all. I didn't know what was going on, but I felt that the children were not being supervised enough at those times. I hoped that this was all just a mistake and that things would get better, but for now, I was overwhelmed at the thought of it all.

One morning soon after that, as I was getting the children ready for pre-school, Katerina came to me crying about something that I thought was a tummy ache. I knelt down in front of her and tried to find out exactly what was wrong. She told me that she was hurting inside. I asked what she meant by that, but she wouldn't say anything more. She just put her little hand between her legs and held herself and cried. I knew then that it was more than just a tummy ache. I had to face the reality of it all now and be strong for my five-year-old daughter. I gave her some pink medicine and I hugged her and dried her tears. I plainly told her that we would talk about it more when she came home from school.

As soon as I put her on the little blue school bus for pre-school though, I ran inside and broke down in tears. How could God allow such a terrible thing to happen to my children! Now all that the psychologists told me had made sense. I had to do something to help my children. The only way to put this to a stop would be to bring it up in court. I would see to it! I didn't care how long it took or how much money it would cost, but I was going to try to put a stop to it all. I got my emotions settled down and I made some phone calls to my lawyer and to the psychologists to find out how to proceed.

Through the many months of hearings and testimony, it seemed as though the stress might take a toll on all of us, but we somehow struggled through. I sometimes wondered if it would eventually be worth it all in the end. I especially hated having to make the decision to put my little girl on the stand to testify, but after that, the judge finally made his decision. He ruled to terminate the overnight stays, even though no one was directly accused. Through all of the testimony, the judge knew that something disturbing was happening to them, and that it was taking place while the children were away from their home. But my lawyer couldn't actually prove anything. But at least with the strict limitations, I knew that they would feel safer sleeping at home. Through all of the turmoil though, they still were allowed to be there unsupervised, but only during the day. At least the battle was worth it in the end, because they were never harmed again.

At home I was struggling financially to pay the utility bills, keep food on the table for us, and keep the children in therapy. I had to find a way to get extra money because the child support just wasn't enough to pay for everything; so I baked bread every week and exchanged it for other food items from my neighbors. I also cleaned house weekly for some of my family and friends for gas money. I was good at cutting hair and giving perms, because I learned that from being in my mother's beauty shop; so I was always ready to help a family member or neighbor out with their hair when they needed it. In exchange, they would bring food or something for the house to help out. I applied and was accepted for welfare and received food stamps and was even able to get WIC coupons, although I had a college degree! I felt pretty bad about it though. Before all of this, I was a teacher with a decent income; and now I was accepting government help to raise my children! It was degrading for me, but I had no choice at the time. My sister Giada would always check my refrigerator when she was over, but there were times that I wouldn't let even her know how much of a struggle it was for me. My good friend and neighbor Jackie noticed how little we had one time, and bought us a couple of chickens at the market, and brought us some vegetables from her garden to help us out. It was hard sometimes to get the child support money every week. Sometimes, there would be several weeks in between payments, and that made it hard to buy food or pay bills. I was blessed though, with wonderful friends and family that would help us and I thanked God for them every day.

Necessity brought out the creativity in me. If I didn't need it, I wouldn't buy it. I didn't want the children to feel needy and poor, but at the same time, I felt sorry for them and wanted to make them happy. It was quite a struggle for me at times, but I cut corners in other ways. I made everything from scratch. I never bought a cake mix or a ready-made dinner entrée. Except for toilet paper, I never bought paper towels or napkins or even tissues. I used cloth napkins and always laundered them to save money. I never bought steak or fancy cuts of meat either. It was always hamburger or chicken or pork for dinner, and lots of pasta. I just varied the way I cooked it with many different recipes.

Garage sale items were a blessing, but if I couldn't find it, I would make it. The curtains were all sewn and fashioned from sheets because I could get more fabric for my money that way. I covered the worn fabric on the couch with new material from the remnant bins at the fabric store. I made pillows to match the couch as well. Thankfully, little dresses and slacks for the kids were easy to come by at garage sales. I even took old socks from my brother-in-law and cut and sewed them to fit Kyle's little feet. The kids never knew where things like that came from because they would be at pre-school when I was busy sewing or looking for clothes for them to wear. Most of the children's apparel was very inexpensive at garage sales. Many things looked almost new or hardly worn. If I couldn't afford something though, my family would always come through with it for us. I remember the bikes I got for them. I borrowed the money from my brother-in-law to buy them new bikes for their birthdays. I was so excited for them because of the city sidewalks and the paved streets; bicycles would be great fun and exercise for them. I paid my brother-in-law back little by little when I had a few extra dollars. He never complained about my debt to him. I borrowed money from him for Christmas presents also, but I paid that back eventually too. I just didn't want the children to feel deprived of anything. My mother and sisters would also see to it that the children had good shoes and nice-looking coats for winter. But toys for Christmas were hard to afford sometimes. I wanted to make their Christmas times joyful, so again I had to figure out how to get the things that they wished for. I didn't have any trouble picking up those little pony dolls for Katerina at garage sales. They could be cleaned up easily and then they would look like new. My sister also gave me one of her daughter's toys for Katerina. It was a pink baby buggy for her dolls. I cleaned it up and it looked like new. Katerina had no idea that it was a hand-me-down when she found it under the tree Christmas morning. Kyle's wish list was a little harder to accomplish though. I remember taking a three-foot tall Bugs Bunny garage sale item, and turning it into an Inspector Gadget doll for Kyle one Christmas. It was going to be a real happy Christmas for them both that year.

When the children got on the little bus for pre-school, I would get busy creating things. Since our major department store downtown was closing because of the mall, I took advantage of some great buys of clothes and shoes for the kids; and some of the items I used to make the Inspector Gadget doll. Everything was only a dollar an item! Besides pants and shirts and shoes for the kids, I found some little blue pants and an undershirt and little black shoes for the doll. I even found a little hat and a tie to fit the doll I was making. I bought some inexpensive gray material at the fabric store and I fashioned a little raincoat for the doll that looked just like the one on the cartoons. I also bought some flesh-colored knit fabric and designed the doll's hands and face with it. I used cotton batting to shape the features underneath the material. Simple thread worked his protruding nose and bulging eyes. When I had finished designing the Gadget doll, I took a picture of it. I sent the picture along with a letter to the company that makes Inspector Gadget toys and asked if this larger size Inspector would be a possibility for them to market. Surprisingly, a box of Inspector Gadget toys, along with a letter from the company, was left on our porch right before Christmas! The company congratulated me on my creativity even though they didn't use my idea, but presented Kyle with a delightful Christmas present.

That Christmas morning also brought another surprise on the front porch. It was a gift basket of food, clothes, and toys for the kids from our church. I didn't know that it showed that much that we were a needy family. My pride was washed away though, as we all delved into the box. It was a happy Christmas for all of us that year, in spite of what we had gone through so far.

Spring the following year brought another setback and pain in my heart for Kyle. It happened on one nice sunny afternoon. While I was waiting on the porch for the children to return, they were late as usual. It was almost dark when they finally arrived. They got out of the truck and bounded up the steps to the door. But when I saw Kyle's face, my mouth dropped. He had a bruise and a welt on his cheek the size of a golf ball! I screamed at him with uneasiness, asking the two of them what had happened! Kyle only replied that he was playing at the park and ran into the slide. I asked him again and again but he repeated the same thing. Katerina also confirmed what he replied. I just didn't understand how he could have actually run into a swing set or slide like that and got such a terrible bruise. He looked a little dazed and I checked his pupils to see if they were both the same size. I was worried that he might have a concussion, so I took him to the emergency room. I was thankful that we lived just a few blocks away from the hospital. The doctor that examined him had an x-ray taken just to make sure that his cheekbone was not fractured.

Although he was all right, and there were not any signs of a concussion, his story didn't make any sense to the doctors either. They had to report this accident to the Child Protective Services because of the extent of his injury. It was standard procedure. I did make sure that it was stated in the report that the accident happened while the children were away, and not in my care. I didn't want to be blamed for the incident, but to my surprise I guess I was.

Just a few days later, I was visited by a caseworker from Child Protective Services. They had received a report from the hospital but the report never stated where the incident took place or who was caring for the children at the time. Kyle and Katerina would not confirm anything to the caseworker either. They were afraid of saying anything at all because they didn't want to cause anyone any trouble. This made the whole incident questionable. I told her that she was barking up the wrong tree, and that the kids were not with me when this accident happened, but because I was the one who brought Kyle to the hospital, she didn't believe my testimony. Here I was only trying to make sure my child was all right, and now my whole teaching career was in jeopardy. They surely would put this incident on file somewhere so that the school system would have access to it. I knew then that it would be fruitless for me to try to get into a public school now, with a battered child incident on my record! I'm sure someone was laughing at me now, but I couldn't do anything about it. I just hoped that I would be able to find some other type of employment that would support us enough to live comfortably some day.

Because we were living in the city now, I thought I would take advantage of some of the activities that were provided in the spring and summer months. The first sport for Kyle and Katerina's age group was T-ball. I enrolled them both on separate teams and looked forward to watching them play ball. Each team's sponsor provided the uniform shirts and hats. The city provided all the sports equipment for the teams. This would be a good experience for them because they would have a chance to interact with other children their age.

My sister Giada and her daughter Rochelle stopped by one afternoon to visit before their games began. The kids were really excited to show off their new T-ball uniforms and hats to them. As Rochelle helped Kyle put on his new cap though, she noticed something wrong with his right eye. She thought it looked like he had a lazy right eye because it was drifting to the outside. I wasted no time, and got him in to see the best ophthalmologist in town that week. He confirmed that Kyle did have a lazy eye, but it was caused by a nerve in the eye, and not by the muscles around the eye. The doctor thought that by wearing a patch over his normal eye, the lazy eye would correct itself. Needless to say, poor Kyle had to wear that darn black patch even during his T-ball games. He enjoyed wearing it though because he could pretend he was a pirate. It made it so hard for him to throw or catch the ball though, using only one eye. The coaches were also disappointed because Kyle could really pitch the ball well. He had a lot of strength in his throw. He just couldn't aim because of the patch. At the first game of the season, most of my sister's family came to watch with me. Because we were all watching him, Kyle was so nervous that when he was up to bat, he ran in the wrong direction around the bases! Everyone laughed at him to make matters worse. He began to cry and I felt so bad for him. This one bad experience confirmed his hatred for any kind of sports from then on. He never wanted to play or watch any sports event again after that.

At the end of that summer, I had to try to enroll Kyle in kindergarten at the elementary school close by. The school set up a morning where all the children who turned five came in to enroll. I was excited about it for him and he was nervous about what to expect. While I was filling out the paperwork, Kyle was supposed to sit at another table and color a picture there with the crayons they provided. He started out fine, but then seeing all the new faces of children and people he didn't know seemed to upset him. He became unruly and started scribbling with the crayons on the table and then broke them and threw them around the room! When I saw him misbehaving, I went over to him, but the principal of the school followed me. He plainly told me that Kyle was not ready for kindergarten and to take him home. At first I was a little upset, but then I thought about it. I realized then that both Kyle and Katerina would be in the same grade if I agreed to hold Kyle back. This made sense to me. They could be together and it would be easier for both of them, so we went back home.

On Kyle's next visit to his psychiatrist, I told the counselor what happened. It was suggested then that Kyle be put in the emotionally disturbed pre-kindergarten class at the Intermediate School District. I went along with the advice and enrolled him there. I didn't want to go against anything that was recommended because all I wanted was help for my son; and if this would help, then I would do it.

After several weeks there, Kyle started showing improvement and I was glad that I put him in the class. The teachers and aids there were very nice and helpful to Kyle. I was able to come and observe him in his class without being seen so it gave me some assurance. They also asked that I set up an appointment to have one of their caseworkers come to see our home. I planned the meeting in November, and thought nothing about it, but when the man arrived, the chaos began. At the time, I happened to be sweeping the kitchen floor. While I was trying to talk with the man, Katerina took the broom and began to run around the house with it while Kyle followed her screaming. The Christmas tree was already up and decorated, but I hadn't moved it close to the wall yet. So Katerina and Kyle began running around the tree and batting the glass ornaments with the broom! Broken ornaments went everywhere while they just kept running around the tree and laughing. They evidently were playing in the land of Oz, and she was the Wicked Witch of the West and he was the Tin Man chasing after her. What a sight! The caseworker could see that I had my hands full with two children totally out of control. After seeing this, he recommended that Katerina also be placed in the ISD classroom.

Now, both of them were in an emotionally impaired classroom there at the ISD, but in different rooms with different teachers. Since I had more time then, without them at home, I volunteered to help out in their classes. It was a rewarding experience for me, observing them and helping out in their rooms.

With Christmas approaching, and shopping to be done, I was getting the feeling that I was falling behind schedule though. I had to help my mother out with her Christmas decorations and also help her shop. I had my decorations up but I didn't have all the presents bought or wrapped. It definitely was the busy season for me that year. It was also a tragic Christmas season for my family—one that all of us will never forget.

My mother was ill for several years and was on a portable oxygen tank with a trachea for about four months. She would never agree to a nursing home, so my sisters and I had to check on her daily and make sure she was getting along all right. I knew that her health was failing, but I was so busy with my children and the divorce and counseling, that I didn't really see how sick she truly was becoming. I called her every day and at least got over to see her a couple of times a week. I figured as long as I could talk to her on the phone every morning, I knew that she was all right. But when she didn't answer the phone one day, I became a little worried.

I was just over to see her the night before and she wanted me to trim her hair, but I forgot to bring my scissors. I told her that I would be over in the morning to cut it. My sister Giada also called her that morning, and she didn't get her to answer the phone either. Giada called me then and said to get on over there fast. I was getting frantic. I drove as fast as I could, praying all the way there. But when I got there, the doors were still locked. I had a key so I let myself in. I walked through the house calling her, but there was no answer. Then I saw her. She was lying on her back in the middle of the hallway, with her arms outstretched. She still had her yellow nightgown on. The bathroom light was on and the faucet was on running water. Her oxygen machine was on in her bedroom but her trachea tube was in her hand. She must have been choking in the middle of the night and went to the bathroom to clean the trachea tubing. I guess I didn't really understand what I was seeing, because I thought she needed oxygen. I dragged the machine over to her and put the mask over her mouth and kept telling her to breathe. Just then her neighbor from across the street came in with the ambulance attendant right behind her.

When I saw him, I yelled, "Do something for her!"

The man knelt down beside her and checked for a pulse and heartbeat, and looked up at me with sadness in his eyes.

I yelled at him again, but he just looked at me and quietly told me that there was nothing that he could do for her because she was gone.

I didn't understand. She was dead? She was gone? That was it? I must have been in shock.

Then the attendant told me that she must have been lying there for about eight hours because her body was already cold.

Here it was three days before Christmas, and now what were we supposed to do? I couldn't believe it. I looked across the room at her little Christmas tree, all lit up with her presents wrapped under it, and sobbed. She must have wrapped them all by herself. How sad it was. I felt so guilty that I didn't get over there the night before to trim her hair.

Maybe I would have noticed then how sick she was, and I could have taken her to the hospital in time. How would we get through this Christmas now? It was supposed to be a time of cheer and happiness, but not for us now. We had to go through a funeral instead and I had to tell my children that their grandmother had gone to heaven.

I thought about the last time that we had her in the emergency room several years before. She almost died then, but we told the doctors to do everything they could to revive her. At least she had those last few years with us and with my children. I remember her telling me when she felt better, that she almost died on that emergency room table that day. She told me how she saw a very brilliant white light and she traveled through a tunnel to the other side. She told me that an angel in a brilliant yellow gown held her arms outstretched and told her to go back. The angel told her that it was not her time and that she was still needed on earth then. I thought it was kind of odd back then, but now when I found her lying on the floor, I realized she was in a yellow gown too, with her arms outstretched just as she had described the angel to me! I guess God knew that I needed her those few years while my children were young and I was going through the divorce.

She really helped me out so much with the kids before they went to pre-school. I remember Katerina was so excited when she was with Grandma and the meals on wheels would come to bring Grandma her lunch. She would always share it with Katerina, even though it really was for my mother alone. I couldn't have made that move to be on my own without her support. It was really going to be hard for me without her, but harder for me to have to tell the kids that Grandma was gone.

I had to make several phone calls to some of my family members. The children had already left and were not in my care, so it was agreed that they would stay there through the funeral Christmas Eve, and be brought back home some time Christmas Day. They would have to stay there overnight. I would tell the children when they came home that afternoon about their grandmother.

It was a very snowy and cold weekend for the funeral and my sister's home out in the country had lost power. I told her to bring her family over to my house and we would all have dinner together and wait for the children to come home. That way, my sister could be there and help me tell the kids about Grandma; and also stay warm while they waited for the power to come back on at her place.

We waited and waited for the children to return, but they didn't arrive until late that night. It was bad enough that they missed spending any time Christmas Day or Christmas Eve with me, but now I had to tell them about their grandmother, so late in the evening. Their Christmas with my family was a sorrowful one—any way you looked at it.

My mother was gone, but she must have wanted me to know that she would still be near me at times. One such time was about a month after she passed on. It was close to 11:00 p.m., but I was still up. I couldn't sleep. The kids were sound asleep, but I was sitting up in my bed and watching a late night talk show. Suddenly I was aware of the smell of the perfume that my mother always wore. It was an expensive perfume, but I really didn't like it at all. That must have been why I noticed it so intensely. The smell of it was permeating my entire bedroom. I also felt a warmth come over me from my waist up, and my face felt like it was burning from the warm sun of a hot summer day. Suddenly, out of the corner of my eye, I noticed a bright glowing light in the hallway by my bedroom door. It filled the hallway with light, just as if it were daytime! But through the light, I could make out an image of a woman standing there in a yellow gown! She seemed to be smiling at me, and her arms were outstretched towards me. I knew then that it was my mother letting me know that she was in heaven and watching over my children and me. It gave me peace and comfort to know that she would be near, but that she was also happy and filled with the love from God.

Seeing my mother made me remember what my aunt Mary told me about what happened when my father died. She was the only one in the hospital room with him at the time that he passed away. My mother just left the room, knowing that it was the last time she would see him alive. But my father asked my aunt Mary to stay with him a little while longer, so she did. He had a type of lymphatic cancer that caused his right arm to swell to the point that he couldn't move it at all. He suffered great pain from it for many weeks before the cancer finally invaded his entire body and took his life. But right before he died, my aunt said that my father saw Jesus! She said that he was so excited about seeing Him that he yelled for her to bring his sketch pad, so that he could draw the face of Jesus. My aunt said that the my father raised his right arm up high and began to draw with tremendous excitement, even though he had been unable to move that arm for many weeks! It was just as he finished the quick little sketch that he took his dying breath and peacefully passed on. That memory has been very dear to me my entire life because I was only eighteen months old when my father died. I really couldn't remember him at all without the stories that my family always told me about him. They made sure to remind me of just how much my father really loved me, even if it was only for those eighteen months.

Hopefully, this New Year would bring emotional healing for us all. After a few more months, the kids would be through with the school term and we could try to bring back some happiness into our lives. Both of them were evaluated by their teachers and psychologists, and improved enough to be put back into the elementary school by our house. This was a positive step for them, and I was relieved. But at the meeting I had with Kyle's teacher, I was informed that he would be at the regular elementary school, but still be in the impaired classroom! They made their recommendations on all the evaluations and I had to sign papers that would allow him to continue in their program, or not at all. They wouldn't give him a chance to be a normal kid in a normal classroom. He was going to be labeled—"impaired"—and I had to agree to it by signing papers. It was like signing papers to have my son committed! I was so upset, but if I didn't sign, they wouldn't let him go to the public school at all! They only agreed to let Katerina go to a regular classroom. Now the children wouldn't be together as I had hoped and planned.

There was nothing I could do about it then, so I signed the papers. I figured that I still could observe him in this classroom, and that would be an advantage for me. I hoped that he would only need to be in there a little while, and then he would improve enough to be put in a regular classroom.

This time, Kyle had a man for a teacher. His name was Mr. Bryant. He was a tall man, with a kind face, and was very soft-spoken. I was sure that he would be helpful to Kyle. I thought that if he could deal with Kyle in a positive way, he might change Kyle's behavior. Since Kyle seemed to dwell on the negative so much, maybe this man might make a difference if he could build up Kyle's positive side. I learned from Kyle's psychologist, just telling him he was a good boy all the time would change his thinking about himself. So I constantly told him how good he was, over and over, every single day. I really felt that it was working too. But when I went to observe him in class, Kyle was standing in the corner in "time out" for something he had already done wrong. Kyle was really testing Mr. Bryant and thriving on the negative attention that would result from his actions. This was still the first few weeks of school, and I could see that this just wasn't right for Kyle. He would go right back to square one if I kept him in that class. I talked to Mr. Bryant about it and I told him that I felt his class just wasn't going to work for Kyle.

So the next week, I pulled them both out of the public school and decided to place them both into the parochial school at our church. I didn't know how I was going to pay for it, but I knew it had to be better for both of them right now. At my meeting with the principal, I agreed to teach music to the elementary school children and also work in the school's library, in exchange for paying tuition for their education. This would be good, because I would be there in the same building with them while they were at school. The only drawback was that I would be teaching them music as well. The school also supplied their uniforms for free, even though they were used ones that had been returned. They really didn't look bad at all. I just had to clean and press them. All I had to buy were white shirts and blouses, and new black shoes for them both, and I knew exactly where to go for the shoes.

There is a tradition in our family that every child had to be fitted for their first pair of high tops and their first pair of school shoes at the old shoe store downtown. It had been there even when I was a child, so I had to take them there, even if it was the most expensive shoe store in town. Katerina picked the most adorable pair of Mary Janes with the embossed toe and buckle straps. Kyle picked the traditional oxford-style shoe that laced up, but with his short, wide feet, they were quite costly. At $35 back then, they were twice the price of Katerina's, but I didn't care. I had to have them. I wouldn't buy anything more that month, except for food. I could manage my money and I would scrimp somewhere else to make up for it. I just wanted to make them happy and as excited as I was for their move to this new school.

After a couple of weeks, the kids had adjusted to their new teacher and classes. Teaching vocal music was easy for me too, because the younger children were very receptive to music and singing. Kyle and Katerina had a real sweet teacher who was very sympathetic to a child's needs, besides making their learning environment very exciting. I remember how proud they were when they came home one day and could recite the alphabet backwards! They thought they were so special because the other kids in the neighborhood couldn't do that. Katerina was actually the first one in her class that could say it all correctly. I knew then that taking them out of the public school was the right thing to do. Kyle was happy and excited about learning from Ms. Brown and so was Katerina. She was such a fun and enthusiastic teacher.

While they were learning about the Pilgrims and Indians before Thanksgiving, Ms. Brown brought in homemade Indian bread with honey that she served to the class. She was always doing special things like that for the children. But even though she was a fun teacher, she didn't let them get away with anything. She told the children that she had eyes in the back of her head so that she could watch them at all times—and they actually believed her! They dared not try anything, because she would see it. Kyle of course, still tried to get away with something once, but she caught him. She began to have him convinced of her special sight. She even told him that she had x-ray eyes and could tell what color of underwear he was wearing! She had tricked him and he finally believed her and started to behave. I think Kyle became her little project though, and she was determined to turn his behavior around. He was special to her.

One day, he had an accident, and messed his pants in class. I don't know if he was actually sick to his stomach or had diarrhea. But Ms. Brown took him out of the class, cleaned him up and actually washed and dried his clothes! She wouldn't let anyone know what happened to him either, because she didn't want Kyle to be embarrassed. The other children in the class thought that he was sent to another class to help with an art project. Katerina didn't even know what had happened. Ms. Brown actually protected him from a devastating emotional setback. This caused Kyle to really appreciate and love his teacher. From then on, he would do his best in her class. I never knew why Kyle had become such a fine student with Ms. Brown until years later though. It was when I happened to see her in a store downtown, and we stopped to talk to each other. She told me then what really happened. I was so grateful to her. She really was a special teacher. She knew just how to handle him, and both Katerina and Kyle liked being in her class.

The semesters went by too fast though, it seemed. Their report cards showed improvement in almost all subjects. They both loved music, of course, but Kyle excelled in it and in art as well. He loved to draw and it seemed that he took everything in like a sponge when it was something he was interested in. He would sit at his little table in the living room for hours with a pencil and a sketch pad and draw and draw. His psychologist said that Kyle was obsessive compulsive, and I could really see it firsthand now. When he was interested in a subject, he would delve into it and have difficulty stopping. That was true for him in reading, when it was a subject he liked, also with music, art, and history. I was quite impressed with his knowledge of history at times, because he would have no trouble remembering historical dates, but the poor kid seemed to have a true mental block when it came to math. But the two of them would help each other out. What he couldn't figure out in math, Katerina would know, and when she would have trouble in history, Kyle would help her. The two of them were like twins, even though they were a year and two days apart. They were very close to each other, always taking the other's side to get the other one out of trouble. It seemed that I could never win a battle with them because the two of them were always sticking up for each other. When Kyle would tease and torment Katerina, she would scream and cry, because she hated to be teased, and Kyle knew it. He knew how to press her buttons, as well as he did with me or anyone else. He was still thriving on negative attention at times, but I really could see an improvement in his self-esteem. He was becoming a happy little boy.

At Halloween, he wanted to be the Tin Man from *The Wizard of Oz*, and Katerina wanted to be Dorothy. Her costume was easy to put together, and of course we had Toto, with our Scotty dog. For Kyle's costume, I had to make a few cardboard pieces that I covered with aluminum foil, and then put them together with duct tape. It worked out well because duct tape was also silvery gray in color. I made him a cardboard axe to go along with it too. He was thrilled with his costume and he would stand and sing the song of the Tin Man with ease. Of course, he remembered every line from the movie, so that was easy for him. I took them to our library in town for a Halloween costume party there, and Kyle won first place with his costume, but Katerina was jealous because her Dorothy came in third place. Walking downtown to our city library was always a fun thing to do. We would even bring the dog along sometimes, and take turns staying outside with him. Those sure were happy days for all of us.

Kyle looked forward to his next school year with anticipation. He enjoyed his kindergarten class with Ms. Brown and thought he knew what to expect with the next school year approaching. However, things weren't always the way one would expect them to be. The first-grade teacher there demanded much more of her class. There were reading and math skills that the children had to be tested on and certain skill levels that had to be met for their age group. First grade was a big step for all of them with their classes lasting a full day now; not a half day like in kindergarten.

Ms. Sinclair was a tall woman with blond hair and the biggest, beautiful blue eyes you ever did see. Kyle and Katerina both remarked that she reminded them of their grandma and I thought so also when I met her. Kyle really loved his grandma and always thought of her as being very sweet, kind, and easy to manipulate. But in no way was Ms. Sinclair anything like their grandma! Ms. Sinclair would catch him every time he tried to cross over her line and she didn't even need eyes in the back of her head to see him misbehave! Kyle, as I have said before, always tried to press a person's buttons, to see just how much he could get away with. Well, Ms. Sinclair stopped him every time, and eventually he gave up trying. He was becoming a pretty good student in spite of himself. He just was terribly messy and unorganized.

It seemed that it was because he was always distracted with his fantasies. If he would have left that part of himself at home, and not delved into his fantasies at school, he wouldn't really have had any trouble there. But he would always do something to draw attention to himself, and it usually was negative attention; like when he dressed up as Mr. Banks from *Mary Poppins* for the Halloween party at school that year.

Kyle dressed as Mr. Banks from the movie *Mary Poppins*

Everyone in the class had no idea who Mr. Banks was, even though I'm sure they all saw the movie. The other children made fun of him and laughed at him behind his back about his costume and how he was acting. He had to wear his suit and somehow I was able to find him a boiler-type hat, along with a cane and of course, a mustache. He even took an old pair of my glasses and took the lenses out of them and attached a cord to one end, and pinned the other end to his vest pocket. These were his spectacles that he would put up to his eyes when he read something in class. Of course, he also used a very believable British accent! He really was very entertaining at times, but the other children thought Kyle was very "weird," so they didn't really want to play with him much. Kyle was just fantasizing about Mr. Banks so much because in the movie, Mr. Banks was the "father figure" that eventually realized he should have spent more time being with his children rather than working at the bank. I think Kyle was wishing that something nice like that could have happened to him. This only made me feel even more sorry for him and guilty for the divorce making his little heart break so much. I wish I could have changed things and not had to go through the divorce, but it seemed the only way to keep my sanity, and to keep Kyle and Katerina from also becoming an emotional wreck.

I remember Kyle coming home one day being pretty upset with Ms. Sinclair. He told me that she had overturned his entire desk because it was so sloppy! He couldn't even find his homework from the night before or the book that he was supposed to be using at the time. She certainly knew how to put a stop to his messiness! One thing he sure hated was to have to clean up after himself, so that did the trick. It took him a little while, but he had to put everything back properly in place. He knew he would have to keep his desk organized from then on. He finally decided that he had to buckle down and become a good student if he wanted to get along with Ms. Sinclair, and he really wanted her to like him.

On the other hand, Katerina had no trouble adjusting to Ms. Sinclair's class. She was a model student from the start and never gave her teacher any trouble. Sure, there were times when they might act up or get a little out of control, but they were still kids, and it generally was expected. However, Kyle always seemed to do something that was unforgettable.

I remember this incident only because of how costly it was to me. I don't know what caused him to do it, but it was unfortunate for me and for him as well. It was close to the end of their second school year, and as Kyle and some of the other boys were playing outside for recess, he somehow managed to lose one of his expensive black school shoes! Katerina told me that she saw them all playing and throwing their shoes up in the air. They wanted to see how high they could throw them, but the only problem was that Kyle threw his up over the schoolyard fence and out of sight. At first, no one could figure out where his shoe went. The whole class helped to look for it, but no one found it, so they all finally gave up. He came home that day without it. It wasn't until several years later that someone noticed a shoe up on the roof of the house next to the playground! Ms. Sinclair called me about it then, but he already had outgrown it.

As that school year went by, I decided that I needed to make a change for myself. I decided to take a few night classes at the community college nearby. I felt that I could better myself with a few computer classes, and maybe get into an office situation. It was not surprising to me that I enjoyed working on a computer and it was easy for me to learn and understand. I just felt like I wasn't getting anywhere teaching music in a parochial school, because the pay just wasn't much at all. With an office job, I would be able to make enough money to give my children and myself a better life. I was still working at the school library and teaching music classes part-time during the day, but when the school year was over, I would look for a different job. Even though Kyle had that playground incident, for the most part, he had improved steadily and matured enough to go back to the public school. That would also be better for me financially, because it was free. I was sure they wouldn't turn him down this time. Katerina would also benefit from the change to the public school. The reading and math programs there were more advanced because of their abundant funds to purchase the latest books and teaching aids; and they both needed all the help they could get in those subjects. This would be a good move for all of us.

Chapter Three

Fantasies

Enrollment in the fall went smoothly for them at the public school, but the kids were placed with different second-grade teachers and in different classrooms. I saw Katerina's teacher first, and she looked like she would be an enjoyable teacher to have. When Katerina saw her, she was delighted. However, poor Kyle was not too happy to see his new teacher. Rather than smile as her new students entered her classroom, she kept a very stern look on her face that made everyone a little uneasy. I wasn't sure how this situation would work out for Kyle. I knew by her appearance though, that Kyle would not be trying to test his limits in her classroom. She really scared him, and I was uneasy being around her myself. I wanted to just see how things went with him, and if there were to be any trouble, I would try to take him out of there. I didn't want any more setbacks now.

I really tried hard to find a teaching job before the fall term, but nothing was available in our school system at that time, so I kept taking computer classes at the community college. They had a good placement program there, and it was free for anyone who was enrolled there. I checked the openings every time I went to class in the hopes of finding something, but nothing came through; so I volunteered to help out at my children's school during the day. My classes were at night, so I was available to help in Kyle and Katerina's computer classes every other day. It was very refreshing to see all the smiles on their faces, as the children came into the computer lab. They were very excited to learn how to use the computer; and the school supplied several reading programs and educational games that the children could use while they were in the computer lab.

After a few weeks, everyone settled into the program and quickly began to work quietly by themselves. I was glad that my nephew gave us his old computer when he purchased a new one. Kyle and Katerina were able to continue their computer time at night after they finished their homework. Our community library also had a free internet sharing program that we were able to use. This helped all three of us with our education. The children were able to use the computer like an encyclopedia, looking up anything they wanted to know about history, music and art. I even purchased a few math programs to help Kyle. I only limited the time they spent playing games on the computer because homework came first. I practiced my typing and word processing skills on it also in hopes of finding a new job somewhere.

With all of us keeping busy one way or another, it seemed that time flew by. As long as I didn't hear anything from their teachers, I was content. Surely no news was good news, as they say. Katerina seemed happy and always ready to tell me what happened at school in her class that day. She was very energetic and talkative. As I recall, that was the only thing that got her in trouble at school. Sometimes, she just wasn't focused on her work because she was too busy talking. She was an average student, and that was okay, as long as she was still learning.

Kyle, on the other hand, was very bright, but his emotions and fantasies would sometimes get in the way. His fears of his teacher would make him so nervous sometimes, that it distracted him from actually learning what was required. This would make him just drift off into one of his fantasies and whatever superhero he was obsessing about at the time. His grades started to show this, but he wouldn't let me know why he was having such a hard time. I tried to talk to him and find out what the problem was, but he just couldn't explain, until one day when I was called in by the principal, Mr. Marshall. I had to go and pick Kyle up because the principal said Kyle was distraught and needed to go home. When I got there, Kyle was out in the hall sitting on the floor.

I could tell that he had been crying, because he was sobbing every so often, and his face and eyes were still red. From my meeting with Mr. Marshall, I was told that Kyle walked out of his classroom and asked to talk to the principal himself, because he refused to go back in his class. He told Mr. Marshall that his teacher really embarrassed him in front of the entire class, and he couldn't go back in. That day she called each student up to her desk to hand in their assignment that they were working on in class. When she asked Kyle to come up to the front with his paper, he readily approached her with confidence that he did a good job on the assignment. However, he was quite surprised and very upset when she scolded him about his work. While she was yelling at him about his paper, she tore it up in little pieces and threw it in the wastebasket—right in front of the whole class! Naturally, everyone laughed out loud at Kyle. That is when he burst into tears and ran out of the room. He was devastated, and finding this out, I was also angry. How could she do that to him! How terrible! The poor kid was made to be an example of stupidity in front of everyone in the room. That was not a proper teaching method, as far as I was concerned—not for any child, and especially not for my son Kyle!

I demanded that Kyle be pulled out of her classroom because of this incident, but Mr. Marshall informed me how difficult that would be. He said that there were certain procedures that had to be accomplished to make this move, especially if Kyle's teacher objected to it. It would be difficult for him to reprimand her because she would be retiring after this school year, and he wouldn't want to soil her teaching career. I felt that she was too old and had been burned out long ago, and should have retired years before, but I didn't have any power or control over her and her method of teaching. I was so frustrated with all of them, but I was consoled that much of the school year had gone by already. Mr. Marshall tried to calm my ruffled feathers, and told me he would keep a very close eye on Kyle. He told Kyle that he would let him leave the classroom and come to him anytime he felt the need. That reassured Kyle enough to make it through to the end of the year. I just felt so bad for him, but Mr. Marshall was very sympathetic to Kyle's needs. Kyle took advantage of his offer by visiting his office once or twice a week.

I think that actually Mr. Marshall acted like a father figure to Kyle in doing so, and that was a good thing. Hopefully, his next teacher would be better.

Fortunately, Kyle seemed to enjoy a few subjects in school that year. One of his favorites was still history. He put his artistic ability to good use for a history project that year. Kyle drew a pencil sketch portrait of every United States president and put them into a booklet with each president's name and dates of their term in office under each drawing. It really was quite impressive for such a young student! However, his teacher still had a very hard time giving him any praise at all for the project, but all of his family sure did!

Everything seemed to be falling into place. I noticed a job opening posted at the college that I thought I would ask about at the placement center. It was not a teaching job, but rather an office job at a greenhouse close to my niece's home. It required some accounting and computer skills, but it didn't have an actual typing requirement. That would be a plus for me, since I could only type thirty words per minute. I just completed my first typing class at the college, and my typing speed was not yet developed. I felt confident enough though to try for the job, so I asked the placement center to send my résumé there and ask for an interview. It wasn't quite a week before I was called in for an interview with the owner of the company! During my interview, he told me that I was the seventeenth person that he had interviewed for the position. When I left, I felt that the interview went well, but I thought that I probably wouldn't get the job. But to my surprise, I was hired a few days later! Now, I finally felt that I was crawling out of the hole that I fell into several years ago. Maybe life would finally start to become a little easier for me to bear now. My financial struggle would be a little easier with a full-time job.

Now I would just have to figure out how to handle the work/school situation. There were a few hours that the kids were home from school before I got home from work, so I had to find a babysitter for that time. After talking to some of my neighbors, I found out that another elementary school nearby had a latchkey program or "kids club" that I could enroll them in. This would work out perfectly because I could drop them off there before school in the morning, and the teachers at that school would get them on their bus and transport them to their school. After school was over, they would be bussed back to the "kid's club," and I could pick them up on my way home from work. It was a great program because the ladies there were very helpful with the children. They would either help them with their homework or supervise fun activities for the kids to pass the time. During the summer months, the children were even supervised with lifeguards at the middle school pool, which was close by. It was a great program for the kids. The only drawback was the cost. I ended up having to pay about half of my earnings each week to the "kid's club" for their services, but I had no other choice. That was the price I would have to pay for being a single parent with two young children and an entry-level job position. I just kept telling myself that things would get better each time I would get a cost of living raise.

Second grade was also a special time for Kyle and Katerina at our church. Being Catholic, second grade was the year that the children make their First Communion and get closer to God. Because they both started out at a parochial school, the beginnings of their faith formation had been met, but since I placed them back in a public school, they had to go to religious education one night a week. There were times that I really struggled to get them there on time, but I never let them miss their religion classes. I knew how important it was for them to make their First Communion, and they wouldn't be eligible to make it without the proper religious training. I know that every little Catholic girl always looks forward to getting that pretty little white dress and veil, and Katerina was very excited about that. On the other hand, I don't think Kyle was that excited, except that he got to dress up in a suit; and oh how he loved to dress up! I of course, was worried about how I was going to come up with the extra money to buy them their First Communion outfits, but I figured I would charge them now and worry about paying for them later. So, off to the old department store in town we went, to buy their special outfits. It was the only place in town that had what they needed because they had a huge children's department upstairs. My mother even bought my First Communion dress there, but they were a lot more expensive now. Luckily, my mother preserved my First Communion veil, so I took it out and had it cleaned for Katerina to wear. That made it a very special time for her, because I was able to pass my veil down to her. She liked it also because my veil had a crown made out of imitation pearls. She felt like a princess when she put it on. Kyle got a new white tie and a white shirt to go with his black suit coat and pants, so he was happy.

Kyle & Katerina's First Communion

The only other thing they needed was their rosaries and First Communion prayer books. My mother even saved my little prayer book, so I got it out and showed it to them and we talked about the ceremony with anticipation. It brought back memories of my First Communion day when I was so sick with the measles, but my mother made me take part in the ceremony anyway. I just remember having such a high fever, that I went outside after receiving communion, and threw up! It was an awful day for me, so I wanted to make their day a very special one. At the church, they seemed to be a little nervous and excited about walking in the procession. I can still see Katerina trying so hard to find where I was sitting while she was walking in the procession. She almost bumped into the little girl in front of her because she wasn't looking where she was going! When she did make eye contact with me, she was relieved. Then she turned to Kyle and nudged him and pointed to where I was sitting so he could also see where I was. They were both so nervous and a little scared, but after their Holy Communion, they seemed to relax and understand that they received the body and blood of Christ. After the mass was over, you could see a change in their behavior where a feeling of calm had settled over them. They relaxed and smiled for all the pictures that we took.

Then it was time to celebrate. I planned a nice party after the ceremony, for all my immediate family. Some of my close friends and neighbors also came. We had a lot of lasagna and pizza, several salads, desserts, and many other Italian favorites that my sisters and nieces brought to the party. It was a beautiful spring day and I still have the picture that my sister took of me with the kids all dressed up in their outfits. It was under that beautiful saucer magnolia tree that I planted in our back yard. We were very happy that afternoon, and I was pleased that their First Communion day turned out so well.

Spring and summer was always such a great time of the year for the kids to be outside playing in our neighborhood. Where we lived, there were only a handful of kids that lived near us that were around the same ages as Kyle and Katerina, until we saw a new family move into the yellow house down the street. A few days later, I was introduced to the new kids on the block. They also were a brother and sister and also were only a year apart and about the same age as Katerina and Kyle. The four of them were delighted to be new friends and playmates with each other. This would keep them all out of trouble and happy and content.

The new kids were very nice children and very respectful of adults. One could tell that they came from a good wholesome family with an extensive religious background. I found out later that their family moved up here from the south and that they were Evangelists. The children spent hours with Kyle and Katerina daily, talking about their religion. I thought it was great that they all got along so well and learned about each other's religious beliefs. I thought it would be good for all of them, but eventually, every time that all four of them got together, an argument developed.

It seemed that all four of them couldn't stop trying to persuade each other to believe in and conform to each other's religious beliefs. The new kids learned from their parents to try to evangelize everyone that they came in contact with. In doing so with Kyle, it just made Kyle believe more and more that being a Catholic was the only religion that mattered. Actually, what Kyle learned from them was to evangelize others to convert to Catholicism! At first, I thought it was a little funny, but as Kyle continued his friendship with them, he studied more and more about the history of Christianity and what it actually meant to be a Catholic. I was very proud of him in that respect.

A few months before the start of the next school year, another family moved into our neighborhood with children. This family also was from a broken home like we were. Their mother divorced her husband and moved into a duplex apartment with her two children. She had a girl younger than Katerina and a boy that was about the same age as Kyle. Ned and Kyle would be in the same classroom the next school year. Tracy although younger than Katerina, seemed much more mature, so Katerina and Tracy got along quite well. At times, Katerina would get into an argument with one of the other neighbor girls, and then wanted to play with Tracy alone. I thought that those two girls were completely the opposite, but I guess it helped them to get along.

Ned was also quite different than Kyle's other friends. Ned was loud and obnoxious at times, and there were moments when I felt he was sneaky about what they were doing, but he really was not a bad kid at all. He was always getting Kyle to play some military game with him and another girl in the neighborhood that was a true tomboy. She lived a couple of streets over, so we didn't see her very often.

Anyway, Ned loved to fantasize also, so he and Kyle really got along well. Ned was another history buff, and that kept the two of them re-enacting in military battles from almost every period of history. There were even times when they got the other boys in the neighborhood involved in their episodes. Ned had a full camouflage uniform with the helmet and canteen and several types of guns that really did look authentic. He wanted to fantasize about being a soldier in World War II. But with Kyle's influence, they would try to re-enact episodes from all ranks of the military and other battles from different wars.

Kyle wanted to be a naval officer on an aircraft carrier, or an officer in the cavalry in the Civil War, or even a frontiersman going west with a wagon train. Kyle was simply consumed with history, and loved to pretend and fantasize being in every historical military action that he knew about. This of course, meant that he had to come up with several "uniforms" to fit his fantasy battles. It was one thing to put on a hat or boots or pretend with a coat or jacket, but Kyle wanted things to really look authentic. I'll never forget finding him up in his room one day making his good suit jacket into a naval military officer's uniform! It was upsetting to me, although he was very creative. He took the buttons off the jacket and made it double-breasted and sewed gold buttons on it. Though that was bad enough, he also cut some gold metallic fringe material from a scarf of mine, and fashioned mortarboards with stars on them! He even put gold embroidery designs on the lapels and sleeves to look like a real navy officer's jacket! Even though I was furious with him for ruining his only suit jacket, I had to give him credit for his creativity! It really did look quite good!

During the summer months in our town, there were several historical re-enactments that would take place because of the unique history in our area. One event was a French and Indian battle re-enactment that was performed on the island near us. Kyle begged me to take him to see it, so I agreed and we went.

It was very exciting with Indian teepees and many men dressed as Indians or French settlers or U.S. Cavalry officers. They tried to keep everything there very authentic with a lot of demonstrations and period clothing and supplies. This showed the children just how hard it was for the settlers and the Indians to live here and survive through the hard winters. Both Kyle and Katerina really enjoyed this truly historical re-enactment. Kyle couldn't wait until he was old enough to join in the whole re-enactment organization. He was very outgoing and not afraid to talk to these men about it and show his interest. So, of course when he found a sponsor, I agreed to help him join. I knew it would cost a bit of money, but I felt that it was important enough to him because of his love of history, so I found out what I had to do to help him.

First, I had to order some special material from our museum and a special pattern, to make his uniform pants. I remember it was thirty dollars just for the blue-gray wool material. It was a very difficult pattern to follow, so I asked for help from my neighbor to make it. Gramma Z, as we all call her, was very good at sewing from a pattern, since she made a lot of dance costumes for her girls when they were young. So Gramma Z made the pants for him. He also had to have some special suspenders and a cavalry hat. We got them, along with some boots, at the used clothing store. But when he asked for a sword and sword belt, I drew the line. There was only so much that I could afford, and that was enough to get him started in the program, which was what mattered. I told him that he could earn some money on his own by shoveling snow for some of the older neighbors or raking their leaves. Eventually, he could earn enough to buy what he wanted. I was not going to just hand everything over to him. I felt that if he wanted something like that bad enough, he would have to try to earn it. I had to try to teach him some responsibility.

After several months, Kyle was invited to one of the local Civil War re-enactors' weekend camps. He was so excited about being able to dress in his cavalry uniform and stay over for a whole weekend with the men who performed the re-enacting episodes. Hopefully, they would let him be in one of the actual battles that they were practicing. He tried to save his allowance to buy a sword and sword belt, but it just wasn't enough. However, he did find an old, used sword, at an auction sale that he went to with his dad, in a neighboring town on one of their weekend visitations. It wasn't anything that was worth much, but he cleaned it up and polished it so it looked real nice. He was happy with the sword, but he still wanted the sword belt so he could wear the sword like the other guys did. I told him again that he would have to keep saving his money for it and then he would be able to order the sword belt from one of their catalogs. He agreed to keep saving and so the conversation about it was dropped.

That evening, I drove him to the campgrounds and left him there in the care of his sponsor. He had his duffle bag packed for an overnight stay, but he wore his Civil War uniform to the site. I thought he looked great in his uniform and I was so glad that the pants fit him well; but were still baggy enough so that they would last a while, as long as he didn't grow too fast. I was so happy for him and proud that he was devoting his time to such a nice hobby, instead of being interested in motorcycles or computer games or something I would have to worry about. As I drove home, I thought about how nice it would be to tell people that my son was interested in history and belonged to a Civil War re-enacting group.

When I got home that Friday afternoon, I called my sister and made plans with her and my brother-in-law to go to the battle re-enactment on Sunday. Katerina also was excited to be able to see her brother perform with the group, but on Saturday afternoon, I received an urgent call from Kyle's sponsor. He told me that I had to come immediately to the campgrounds. I asked him what happened because I thought that maybe Kyle was in an accident of some sort, but he wouldn't tell me anything except that Kyle was not hurt. I took Katerina with me and drove there as fast as I could without being reckless or speeding. I didn't want to get stopped by the police because I was already so nervous about the whole thing and worried about what happened.

When I finally got there, I saw Kyle marching around through the campgrounds with a re-enactor that was talking to him about something as they marched. I saw that Kyle kept nodding his head as the man talked to him. I thought that he was being trained about rehearsing a drill or something, but that was not it at all. When I got out of the car, Kyle's sponsor approached me and told me the whole story. He said that Kyle was being counseled because he had stolen an antique sword belt from this man and claimed it as his own! I was told that they were about to call the police and file a report about it, but the man dropped the charges when Kyle gave it back to him and hadn't damaged it at all. I'm sure my face showed the remorse that I felt inside when I heard this news. My heart was broken and I was so disappointed with my son, but at the same time I was so angry with him. I quickly had to think about what I should do to punish him for this embarrassing episode. I couldn't believe it. My son Kyle was stealing? I just shook my head in disappointment as tears rolled down my cheeks. Kyle's sponsor told me to take the boy home, and that he would call him in a few days about his membership in the group, after they had a meeting about it.

Kyle gathered up his belongings and got in the car without looking at me. I could tell he was sorry and he was scared about what was going to happen to him now. There was complete silence in the car as we drove home. I didn't want to talk to him for fear of losing my temper. I knew that I was too angry at the time to try to talk about it. I just kept thinking about what he did and how I was going to punish him, and then it hit me. I was a block away from our church, stopped at the light. Suddenly I decided I would bring him to see our priest. If I had to drag him in there, I would make him talk to our priest and tell him what he did! I was going to make Kyle as embarrassed in front of our priest as I was in front of the camp sponsor! I knew that he wouldn't like that one bit, so I drove up to the church rectory. I didn't even have to look for Father Bob because he was just coming out of the building. I waved for him to wait a minute and we got out of the car to talk. With tears in my eyes, I told Father Bob what Kyle did, and that was all I needed to say. Father took Kyle aside and talked to him alone for a few minutes. Afterwards, he came over to me and told me that he and Kyle would be talking in private for several weeks for counseling. He said that he would call Kyle weekly for a while to check on his status. I was so grateful and thankful that our parish had such a wonderful priest that we could go to when we needed help. I knew he would be able to turn

Kyle around. I knew then that Kyle would never try to steal anything ever again.

After a few days, Kyle was receiving phone calls regularly from Father Bob after school or in the early evening. I don't know what they talked about, but I remember Kyle's attitude changed more and more after each call. It seemed that it didn't take very long for him to become a more humble person, sincerely trying to make amends for what he did. Eventually, Father Bob stopped calling him altogether, and I was happy knowing that my son could be trusted again.

Eventually, I allowed Ned to stop by and hang out with Kyle again. I was pretty sure that I could trust the two of them to stay out of trouble now. They both seemed to be mature enough so I let Ned stop over for a few hours on Saturdays while I was at work. Naturally, they were back into their uniform fantasies of World War II and re-enacting battles. They both started collecting old ribbons and medals for their uniforms now. It all started when Kyle went to a few farm and country auctions in the neighboring towns with his father. He was able to buy several ribbons and medals at very reasonable prices, so it was a good hobby for him to get involved in. There also was an Army-Navy surplus store in a town close by that I could drive the boys to. They talked me into taking them there just about every other weekend, but that was okay. They would have a lot of fun collecting. Kyle totally gave up on his Civil War uniform and the sword belt, so I didn't say anything about it because I was sure he abandoned the idea because he didn't want to be reminded of what happened. The camp director never called him about any more gatherings either, so it was dropped.

These decorative ribbons and medals were supposed to be worn on an army uniform in a specific order, so the boys did their research at the library and on the computer to find out exactly what each ribbon stood for and what medal it represented. They studied them and learned exactly at what place on the uniform that each ribbon should be worn. Kyle was so exact about his knowledge of the placement of the ribbons that he could even spot mistakes in movies where the ribbons were placed incorrectly on the actors' costumes. It was funny at times to watch a movie with him.

He would stare at the television screen and suddenly shout out, "Incorrect! Incorrect!" and with a disgusted look on his face, shake his head negatively.

That really didn't matter to Katerina or me, and we didn't really care, but it made Kyle upset with the movie.

During that school year, I encouraged Kyle and Katerina to try to learn a musical instrument. Since I was a music teacher at one time, I wanted them to see if they liked music as much as I did. So I signed them up for violin, which was the first type of instrument that was offered at their school. I even took them to several free Montessori violin sessions that were offered at our community college. They both seemed to really enjoy playing the violin at first, and Kyle even encouraged a couple of his friends to also join his violin class. He seemed to have a great time with his friends in the class, but the teacher let me know that Kyle and two other boys would rather pretend they were the Three Musketeers with their violin bows, instead of actually playing the violin. At one concert that Kyle was in, I can remember seeing him and Bobby and David on the stage beforehand. All together they shouted, "One for all, and all for one!"

They kept the whole class entertained, but not in the way they should have. Unfortunately, because of their antics, all three of them didn't continue with violin the following year. Katerina didn't stay very enthusiastic about the violin either, but at least she finished the class through to the end of the school year. After the violin attempt, I decided to give instrumental music one more try, so I signed them up for the flute and the trumpet the next year. Katerina enjoyed the flute, but Kyle just wasn't that enthused about the trumpet and so he dropped the class after a couple of weeks. Again, Katerina continued on the flute through the entire school year. But when they went on to junior high school, they both decided to go into vocal music instead. Naturally, I was disappointed, but at least they still would be in a music class of some type.

Along with singing, Kyle decided to try acting as well. I also thought he would do well in that, especially since he still loved to play dress up. The first play that he was in was a real big hit with the audience. It was a simple play that actually was a take-off on *Don Quixote*. As I recall, they were in the sixth grade at the time. The whole play was short and simple, and actually not too interesting, until Kyle's character came on the stage. Kyle was supposed to play the part of a knight that was a little disoriented, simple, and scattered in his behavior. It was a great part for Kyle—especially the scene where he was trying to mount his horse with all his armor on. He kept trying to get on the horse and comically fell off of it three times! He was hilarious and the parents chuckled and laughed out loud. Some parents were actually crying with laughter. He really made the play a great success. I felt so proud of him—especially when many parents in the audience came up to me after the play and told me just how much they enjoyed Kyle's performance. He really was perfect for the part and he played it well. I knew then that Kyle would be a good actor someday, if he continued to perform.

Kyle as a knight in his sixth-grade play

This school year was also a turning point for Kyle in academics. So far, I always worried about Kyle's behavior in class, especially when I got a call from a teacher. I dreaded those parent-teacher nights because it seemed that I was continually making excuses for him and had to explain why Kyle acted the way he did sometimes in class. His sixth-grade teacher was the first male teacher for Kyle in a regular school classroom. I wondered how Kyle would react to him, especially after that pre-school incident. I didn't even think anything of it at first, especially since I didn't hear anything from the principal or the teacher. No news was good news again. Then parent-teacher night came. I just knew I would have to make excuses for his behavior again somehow. When I went in for my meeting with Mr. Branson, I expected the worst. Mr. Branson looked at me and introduced himself and we clasped hands.

He shook his head negatively, but with a questioning smile, and said, "I can't believe it about Kyle."

I said with remorse, "What did he do wrong now?"

Mr. Branson shook his head again and said, "How did you raise such a great kid? How did you do it? He is exceptional!"

I looked at him stunned and confused and said, "There must be some mistake. Are you sure you are talking about MY son, Kyle?"

I was completely astonished! Then he went on to tell me just how GREAT Kyle was. I never heard that before! I was stunned! I didn't know what to say! Mr. Branson told me that in all of his teaching days, he never came across a student as perfect as Kyle was in his class. He told me how Kyle would sit at attention throughout the day and never even go out for recess. He didn't even want to take a break for lunch. He would just sit there right in front of the teacher's desk and work hard all day. Because of it, Kyle had straight A's in all of his work! He was an exceptional student for Mr. Branson! Tears came to my eyes. I finally heard some praises for my son in his schoolwork! Kyle turned himself around and became a fine young man that I could be very proud of. Truly, this year was the greatest achievement for him and I was just beaming with pride. I thanked God for His blessings. Now I could relax knowing that he was finally going in the right direction when he started junior high the next school year.

Chapter Four

Transformations

We were fortunate to live in a city where the largest school system was very near to us. The elementary school was just a couple of blocks away. Transferring to the next grade level meant changing to another school building, but I was glad that it was just four blocks down our own street. Even though we had to get up earlier now for school, the kids could be there in just five minutes by walking. It also made it easy for me to drop them off there on my way to work if the weather was bad. I'll never forget how nervous Kyle was about the change in buildings though. He was afraid he wouldn't be able to find his way around because now they had to move to different classrooms for each subject. It was all part of growing up and experiencing new things and new surroundings. Kyle hated change as much as I did, so I understood and felt badly for him. Katerina wasn't bothered about it at all. It actually excited her that she would be able to move to different classrooms and meet new kids and make new friends.

That first week was really hard on Kyle. I could see how nervous he was, so I asked him if he wanted to tell me what was bothering him. He told me how he had a couple of bad confrontations with some bullies on his way into the building. He said that they were waiting for him by the flagpole each morning, to try to cause him some trouble. He wished that he could find another entrance into the school so that he could avoid these confrontations, but the front entrance was the only door that was open in the mornings. I told him that it would not be a good idea to try to avoid these guys. The best thing for him to do would be to confront these bullies and stand up to them. Running away would never resolve his problems. I told him that he would have to outsmart them by using a little psychology, so we came up with a good plan. Since Kyle seemed to enjoy acting, I suggested that he might try a little acting as he approached the door. Maybe he could outsmart them and make them think he was someone who was not as timid as he was in the past few days. He thought about it and came up with a plan for the next morning. He told me that afternoon that as he passed the flagpole and headed toward the door that morning, he knew they were right behind him. When he reached the door, he suddenly turned around, and with a very strange look on his face he shouted out to them that he forgot his medicine that morning. He yelled out that they might get hurt if they were to provoke him, because he could explode into a violent rage at any minute! He chuckled as he described the looks on their faces when they quickly turned and ran away! I was so glad that he resolved that problem on his own. This was a good start for him at character building and learning to deal with other people. After a few weeks, he settled comfortably into his schedule and began to relax and be his happy old self again.

At home, Kyle and Ned were still collecting ribbons and medals, but now they started collecting uniform hats as well. I knew that on the weekends that the kids went with their father, they would attend several auctions in the area. It could have been possible to find an army helmet or a navy sailor's cap there, once in a while. But Kyle showed me several uniform officers' hats that looked like they were brand new. They had all the gold embroidery on the brims that he told me were called "scrambled eggs." Now, I knew that there was no way that he could have found them at one of these auctions, so I became a little suspicious, and I confronted him about it. One thing I knew was that Kyle could never lie to me. He knew that I could tell by the look on his face if he was not being truthful, so he always gave in and told me everything.

The story was that he and Ned researched the computer and found a web site that actually sold uniform hats. He said he called the company and placed an order over the phone. The only trouble was that he had to own a business to buy from them, so Kyle made up a fake company name and began purchasing these hats! He was so happy about it until he got the statement for his purchases and realized he would have to come up with the money! I couldn't believe that this company would let some twelve-year-old kids place an order with them! Then he told me how he called the company and changed his voice to sound like an older man, and made up a business license number and actually placed the order! The hats were delivered to him through the mail and it was as easy as that. He bought two officer's caps with the scrambled eggs on the brim, and the bill came to $120! I was furious with him and I was sure that Ned had a hand in this also, but somehow he had to pay for them because the company had a no-return policy if the items were worn or used.

I was stuck paying the bill, of course, but I was not going to let him get away with it at all. I took the hats away from him, and gave them to my sister Giada to hide at her house until Kyle saved up the money to pay for them. One at a time, little by little, he earned enough money to get the hats back with the plan I made for him. I made arrangements for him and Katerina to work after school at the greenhouse where I worked. Greenhouses are an agricultural operation, and because of that, if I worked there, then my children could work there part-time as well. They were just at the legal age to start, so my boss agreed to give them some work to help me teach them some responsibility and the meaning of a dollar. They were put with the most experienced head grower there. Anne also was the most caring person, and knew my circumstances, so she gave them extra guidance. Katerina loved the work and was not afraid at all to get dirty pulling weeds or watering flowers. To this day, I felt that she could have made an excellent head grower if I would have let her stay there to work. She would have had to go to college and get a degree in horticulture, and that would be very costly, so I didn't mention it to her.

Kyle, on the other hand, was harder to deal with. He knew he had to be good there and follow orders because he knew I would be furious with him if he embarrassed me there, so he tried to do his best—for a while. He just didn't have the patience or the interest in the job to keep from being distracted. Anne would find him daydreaming and distracted with things most of the time. She had to keep a close eye on him to keep him in line, and I heard about it several times. This did not make her very happy with his performance, so he got lectured quite a bit about it from me. I was not going to give in to him. He had to work to pay for those darn hats! Eventually, when he realized he didn't have a choice, he tried harder and kept at it. Finally, the hats were returned to him, but with another lecture from me, of course.

At one point when they were in their seventh grade, I noticed a tension among them when they went away for one of their weekends. Both of them were coming home not only tired and worn out, but also angry. All I had to do was ask them if they had a nice time, and boy did I regret it! Katerina had a real angry look on her face as she marched out of the room. She wasn't going to say anything at all for fear of getting into an argument with me. On the other hand, Kyle was ready to let me know what was wrong. He told me that he was sick and tired of going because he felt that he was only there to work. It was not fun anymore.

Katerina didn't want to say anything bad, but Kyle told me that they had to work very hard cleaning out houses and boxing up items to get them ready for auctions. Kyle was upset because he and Katerina were expected to work the entire day for the auction that would take place the following week. It was bad enough that they had to work, but they felt that nothing they did was appreciated. Kyle said that at one point, he was kicked in the behind while he was picking up a box, and he tripped and fell over everything. Then he was yelled at even more because he couldn't pick things up fast enough. Kyle felt so degraded. He felt like he was just being used as a type of workhorse, and that was not supposed to be what they were there for at all. He started to cry as he told me about the incident. It was supposed to be a fun time where they could all be together enjoying life and doing fun things. Kyle told me that since he was thirteen already, he wanted to file a grievance with the friend of the court and stop going altogether.

I felt that filing a grievance would only cause both of us trouble, but he insisted that something should be done about it. He also refused to go any more at all. So on Monday, I called the caseworker and set up an appointment for Kyle to tell her what was bothering him. Since he was thirteen, he had the right to file a complaint on his own.

When the day of the meeting finally arrived, I called off work and took him to the courthouse. Waiting outside the hearing room in the hallway made me a nervous wreck, as I recalled being there many times for our hearings. Kyle seemed anxious though to tell his caseworker what was on his mind. When she finally greeted us, she took Kyle in her room alone. I was not allowed to hear their conversation. After an hour had passed, her door opened and the two of them approached me. I was relieved to see them both smiling and laughing as they walked down the hallway. His caseworker seemed delighted that she was able to talk with Kyle. He was always very personable besides being very respectful with adults. He always seemed to get along well with older people, especially women. So when she told me that she understood completely why Kyle wanted to talk with her, I was relieved. She informed me that she would file his complaint and we would be hearing from her within the next week about the court's decision on this matter. I was just glad to get out of there because that place brought back a lot of bad memories for me. It was roughly seven years of court hearings and legal meetings for my divorce to finally be over, but when there are children involved, it never really ends. With every phone call, and every confrontation, and every time they left, I was reminded of the life we once had together, and how bitter we had become. The only thing I kept reminding myself to be aware of, was to never let my kids hear me say anything negative in their presence. I may have felt a lot of anger, but I tried not to show it in front of them. I never felt any regret though. I was sure that I made the right decision after all.

The next week brought news from the friend of the court. Kyle was happy when he opened the letter that stated that it would be optional for him but that Katerina would still be obliged to conform to the schedule. I was glad that it was over and that Kyle wouldn't be in contempt of court if he refused to go after all. I'm sure there was remorse on both sides, but neither of them would apologize, so for the next three years, there was no communication between them—not even on the phone. When a holiday came around though, my sister Giada would call to let him know just how much he was missing out on such a great kid. There would certainly be regrets some day.

So, after several years of silence between them, their anger finally subsided and they began seeing each other again. I don't recall exactly how the ice was broken, but I know my sister had a lot to do with it. I don't think that things were ever really the same between them though. They were both very stubborn.

The rest of the school year went by pretty smoothly. Kyle especially enjoyed being in the junior high school choir and the school plays. Katerina enjoyed playing volleyball and basketball more, even though she did sing in the women's choir. The two of them were becoming just the opposite in everything they enjoyed, but they stayed best friends with the same kids in the neighborhood all through junior high. Ned would always convince Kyle to get involved with every military fantasy that he could devise. He talked Kyle into joining the Civil Air Patrol with him and also got him interested in citizen's band radio communications. Everything was fine until the two of them started messing around with the shortwave bands and would inadvertently reach someone in another country. They knew that they were not licensed to talk on the shortwave, but they did it anyway, until one day they were almost caught and reported. That is when I took the radios away for a while. Eventually, he lost interest in them altogether, but he liked going to the Civil Air Patrol meetings because he could get dressed in his uniform. Besides the actual uniform, I think Kyle stayed in the Civil Air Patrol through high school because he somehow convinced the commander to let him be the chaplain at their meetings. He let everyone he knew in school that he was an officer, being the chaplain. Later on, Ned almost convinced Kyle to join the Air National Guard, but Kyle was worried that he would get drafted if there would be a war some day, so he refused to get involved in it.

Besides schoolwork, their eighth grade was the last year of their religious education classes, and then they would be confirmed in their religious beliefs. It was going to be another milestone in their lives and a time for them to gain some maturity and responsibility in their faith formation. I was excited for them, but I remembered all the struggles and coaxing I did with them when they were younger, just to get them to go to church at times. I would be glad when they would finally have to make their own decisions about their faith. It was also nice to go shopping for new clothes for the occasion. Katerina chose a beautiful green velvet dress that made her green eyes sparkle. I loved to see her in a dress, but there were very few times that she would ever wear one. She would rather just wear slacks for every occasion, no matter how much I tried to persuade her to wear a dress. However, Kyle loved to dress up in a suit. I was more than happy to buy him a new one for his confirmation.

Kyle in his eighth-grade confirmation suit

It was a pretty exciting evening for them both because they would go before the bishop and they would have to answer his questions, if they wanted to be confirmed. I had prepared a little family gathering and celebration afterward and had all the food and refreshments ready. It was going to be a memorable occasion for us all, but especially one for Kyle. I watched them approach the bishop and I saw that Kyle was a nervous wreck. Katerina was a little nervous also, but Kyle actually seemed scared about it all. My sister's youngest daughter, Patrice, was their sponsor. We both sat there in the pew and watched the two of them walk up to the bishop in line side by side. We couldn't hear what was said, but we knew what they were supposed to do and say in front of the bishop. After Katerina was confirmed, I saw her quickly walk back to our pew with a smile on her face and quickly sit down, but when it was Kyle's turn, the bishop took a little longer. When Kyle turned to walk back to our pew, his face was quite red and he had tears in his eyes, but at the same time, he was smiling a great big, beautiful smile. You could see he was filled with tremendous joy.

When he got back to his seat next to me, he told me what happened. I didn't know what to think when I heard him explain his experience. He told me that something really special had happened to him up there. He was so excited. He was whispering, but I could tell that he wanted to shout with joy. He said that when the bishop laid his hands on his head, he felt a great rush of warmth, which actually felt like a fire spreading down through his head and into his chest. He told me that he felt something very special. He was sure that the Holy Spirit had touched him! He was sure that he was called by God in a very special way. I didn't know what to think of his comments. I knew that Kyle was a different sort of kid, and I guess it really wasn't that much of a surprise to me that he would make such a comment. He just was a unique character, and I actually wasn't surprised. But then he told me that he knew now that he was going to become a priest! I didn't know what to say. I guess I was in a little shock from it. Maybe he was just fantasizing. Maybe he was just trying to see what I would say about it. On the other hand, maybe he really meant it. Maybe something very special was really happening to him. I didn't know what to say or what to think. I just knew that Kyle seemed very excited and happy about what just happened to him, but he was only fourteen years old! I wanted to just wait and see how long this feeling would last with him.

In the fall that year, after Kyle and Katerina had another birthday and they were back at school, I let him apply for a work permit. Having a job that paid a little more would help him get the things he wanted, so he got a job in the deli department of the largest grocery chain in our area. It was a fairly new store in our town and he was excited that he would be working with adults and serving customers. In the deli, he helped the older ladies who prepared the salads and desserts, besides clearing tables, stocking refreshments, and keeping the floors clean. It was a lot of work, but he loved helping the older ladies. He carried the heavy containers of food into the kitchen for them and also put the large trays away for them. He had such a charming way about him and the ladies loved him. They complimented him and praised him for his help all the time. This just made Kyle work even harder. He didn't mind it at all. He loved his job and he loved meeting and talking to all the customers that came into the deli to eat. While he was clearing the tables or mopping the floors, he would carry on a lot of conversations with everyone he met. One frequent customer to the deli was a priest. His name was Father Joseph and he would visit the deli just about every day for lunch or dinner. I also knew him from his many visits to the greenhouse to buy flowers for his parish. Father Joseph was quite impressed with Kyle's religious knowledge and enthusiasm at such a young age.

It was just about every day that Kyle told me about his conversations with Father Joseph and their discussion about religion. It was always about the old ways with Kyle, and the Latin Mass and how Kyle wished that Latin would still be used in the services. He wanted everything to go back in time to the days before Vatican II. It was unusual for a young boy to be that knowledgeable about church history, but even more unusual that he wanted to revert back to the old ways of the church practices. After a couple of years, Kyle and Father Joseph became good friends and looked forward to their lunchtime discussions. Kyle had definitely sparked the interest of this priest. So when I received a phone call from Father Joseph several months later, I knew what he was going to tell me. I tried to forget about what Kyle said to me about the priesthood, but now Father Joseph confirmed to me just how serious Kyle really was about it. Father Joseph let me know that he made arrangements at the seminary for Kyle to go there for the weekend discernment if I would give him my permission. He was going to pay all the expenses and sponsor him if Kyle agreed to go.

That next Sunday, I knelt down before Mass and prayed to God about how I should handle this whole thing. I told God that I would let Him have Kyle for the priesthood, if that was His plan for Kyle, even though I didn't want to give him up. I was sad though, that I would never see my son get married or have children of his own for me to spoil. I told God that I would let him go because Kyle was His before he was mine and I reluctantly would not stand in Kyle's way. I wanted Kyle to be happy, even though it would make me sad. I just wouldn't let him know how I felt. So when the time came for the discernment weekend, I agreed that I would take him there. The arrangements were made for the following fall, so that Kyle would have more time to prepare and contemplate about it. For now, he had to concentrate not only on his schoolwork, but he had choir and play practice as well. Kyle really enjoyed singing and was involved in a small vocal group of several of the best male vocalists in the choir. This group not only performed at district and state competitions and received the highest awards, but also performed for our governor on two occasions. He was also in a special group of a dozen male and female students that performed special programs at all the school concerts. He was in the madrigal singers group also, and they dressed in beautiful medieval costumes to perform. That was his favorite singing group because they sang many religious songs and some were even performed in Latin. He loved the language and wished that it would still be used in the Catholic Mass.

Kyle at the madrigal singers performance

He continued acting and had one of the lead parts in the play that year. They were doing *Annie*, and he was going to be FDR. He was so excited about playing the part of the president because he would be wearing an old-fashioned suit and spectacles. He still loved to dress up, of course. Over and over, he practiced imitating the voice of FDR and speaking with a pipe in his mouth. He didn't even mind that he would be in a wheelchair for the play. The only thing that made him a little nervous was the actual lines that were sung alone in front of everyone; but when it was his time to sing, he was great in it. We just had to keep telling him he could do it and build up his confidence. In the end though, he always came through with flying colors. Our family was so proud of him when the audience cheered at his performance. He really did look and sound like FDR and many people there came up to me after each performance to let me know just how much they enjoyed Kyle in the play. I went to every performance and sat right in front where he could see me. I wanted him to know that I would always be there for him.

Kyle as FDR in the play *Annie*

The seminary discernment weekend finally approached. My sister Giada agreed to drive Kyle there with me. She knew the area much better than I did and I really hated to drive, so she took us there. The seminary was a beautiful, secluded old building right in the middle of a very busy area of the city. We had to have special permission just to get into the gated parking lot. Father Joseph called ahead to let the guard know we were coming. We were met at the door by one of the supervising priests who welcomed us and made us feel more at ease. He took the three of us on a little tour of the building and showed us where Kyle would be staying. He explained to us what was scheduled for Kyle to do and introduced us to a few of the seminarians and several priests that were teachers there. Then Giada and I went to the chapel and prayed while they took Kyle to his room and got him settled in. After a while, he came back to say goodbye to us for his weekend stay. Kyle had a big smile on his face and a bit of a tear in his eye when he hugged me and kissed me goodbye. I finally could see how much he had grown up and how serious he was about his decision. It made me feel sad, but I couldn't cry in front of him. I didn't want to make him feel bad, so I held it all in until I got to the car to go home. Giada and I both cried on the drive home. Things were never going to be the same anymore.

When Sunday finally came around, Giada and I drove back to the seminary to pick Kyle up. We were both excited to see how he liked his stay at the seminary and if he still wanted to become a priest. The supervisor met us at the door, and called up to Kyle's room to let him know we had arrived. When he came down the stairs to greet us though, I could tell that something had changed with him, but I didn't want to say anything until we were back in the car.

The ride home was a quiet one. Kyle didn't really have much to say about his weekend visit. He did tell me though, that he felt a little uneasy around some of the other candidates that came for the discernment. Kyle felt out of place because his thinking was so different from the rest of the guys. I thought that maybe he was just not supposed to tell us what went on there, so I didn't press him about it until he and I were alone at home. Then I asked him if he wanted to talk to me about it, and he finally broke down. He was so disappointed. Not only did he feel uneasy there, but his whole idea of life as a priest had crumbled to pieces before his eyes. He simply told me that he didn't want to be a priest anymore. He had made such big plans for himself, and had such big ideas of how he was going to serve God as a priest, and now it was over. The reality of going to the seminary wasn't at all what he thought it would be. He had several conversations about his attitude towards the change in the church, during his meetings with some of the priests and the teachers there. They were impressed with Kyle's knowledge of the Bible and religion, but Kyle's feelings about Latin and his old-fashioned ways were not what they were looking for in the candidates. I really think that if Kyle had been at a seminary in Italy or even in Ireland, he would have felt a lot more at ease, and more likely to fit in. Instead of progressing in this modern age to an all-English Mass, Kyle was digressing back to the times before Vatican II where Latin was used in the Mass. That is what he wanted to try to influence and bring back. He probably would have felt more at home if he lived in Italy where the common language was closer to Latin. But he really thought that he could create a movement here to bring back Latin in the Mass. They must have thought Kyle was very peculiar in his thinking. I guess it was just very unusual and hard to believe that a young man would prefer to live in the past and bring back old-fashioned ideas, instead of conforming and progressing into the future.

So Kyle felt that the seminary was just not for him. He neatly tucked away all of his dreams of becoming a priest, and set out on another plan of action for his future. He would preach the Gospel and evangelize without becoming a priest. He would be a prayer warrior in his own right; even though he didn't want to become a priest anymore, he knew God wanted him still to evangelize in his own way. This was going to be his plan. I didn't know this of course then, but eventually I found out about his plan from his friends and what they would tell me of his behavior, years later.

Outside of school, Kyle also had several job changes. The store had to change requirements for some of the job positions because of age.

This change eliminated Kyle's work in the deli and moved him to outside work, which he hated, so he went to work for another store. This time he decided to work in the paint department of another large chain store in our area. He remembered what my mother told him about my father and how he was an artist and a painter. We showed Kyle pictures of my father painting the outside of a house and told him how my dad made a living out of interior decorating and house painting. Kyle loved art and painting as well, but when I encouraged him to take an art class, it was a mistake. Kyle could really draw, but only with a common #2 pencil. He could do portraits easily when most people found them difficult to do. The art teacher tried to encourage him to use other mediums like charcoal or oil paints, but it just made Kyle drop the class. He wouldn't let any art teacher tell him how to draw or how to paint.

Kyle was very set in his ways. But he must have felt that he wanted to follow in his grandfather's footsteps at one point, because he bought all the equipment and clothes that a professional painter would have used. He was even hired for a few painting jobs in our neighborhood that gave him a few extra dollars. For a while he enjoyed the paint department there, but the pay wasn't very good; so he went on to another department store where he actually managed their paint department. He really enjoyed this job because of the people he met every day and the friendships he developed there. His friends told me that Kyle really took advantage of his situation there as a manager though. They laughed when they told me what Kyle would do.

Since he was in charge of ordering all the paint supplies, he organized the storage room to his own liking and actually set up a little office in there right by the employee lunch room. He was in his glory back there. The store manager even let Kyle do what he wanted with the storage room because everything was neat and orderly in there, and Kyle did a good job at keeping the proper supplies on hand. But it was his little office back there that had everybody chuckling. He was a real sight to see as he leaned back in his chair and acted like he was the boss of the back room. It was not unusual though, to see him every day, with a sandwich in one hand, and his Bible in the other, and his feet propped up on the desk. He read his Bible at lunch there every day.

Behind the scenes, he became good friends with the store's undercover detective that also worked in the back. His name was Sam and he was about the same age as Kyle. He was also a very religious young man, but he was not Catholic. That didn't matter to either of them though, because they talked about religion every day anyway, and how their faith was different but also how it was the same in many ways. Sam was there for several years already when Kyle started working there, so he let Kyle in on a few of his detective secrets. Since the paint department was close to one of the main entrances, Sam had Kyle help him out, observing people as they came and went in and out of the store. When there was a shoplifter detected, Sam had Kyle help him with his undercover work. There were even a few times that Kyle actually caught a shoplifter, but that was because he was able to stop the person after they walked out the door. Then it was legal to stop them. One time, Kyle told me how he actually chased a guy in the parking lot and pinned him down and waited for Sam to come and arrest him. Kyle even got his trousers ripped during the shuffle and chase that time, so the store gave him a brand-new pair of slacks as a reward for his help. He and Sam became very close friends and Kyle worked well with Sam. He loved being undercover, along with selling paint and talking about religion. He was very personable with the customers too. It made me feel pretty good when I would hear from one of my friends or relatives about Kyle. They all told me that they saw Kyle at the store and had such a nice conversation with him. He was a very likable guy and actually stayed there for several years.

During his high school years, Kyle also remained friends with Ned and the two of them continued fantasizing with their pretend police actions, while they rode around in Ned's car looking for trouble. They always said they were going to go BOL-ing—which meant that they were going to "be on the lookout" for any trouble. With Ned's black sedan all souped up to look like an undercover detective car, with a radio and extra lights, they were deep into their fantasies. But one night, it wasn't very much fun. They were stopped by the state police and were actually brought in for questioning! Of course, I didn't find out about it until months later, but they told me that they were labeled as being suspicious characters, because they were caught following police cars several times and interfering with police work! They were able to make a phone call to Katerina and she picked them up because Ned's vehicle was impounded overnight so the police could look it over. He picked it up the next day without any more trouble. I guess it was that incident that finally put a stop to their little covert actions.

Kyle also was good at getting away with things that he really should have been ticketed for, but his charming personality certainly helped him out of trouble. I found out from my cousin who owned a towing company, that he helped Kyle get his car out of a ditch several times when he was driving too fast down those old country roads. Kyle was not very cautious at times and actually rolled his car halfway in a ditch several times, but I never knew about it until years later. My cousin always came to Kyle's rescue and never asked for any payment for his services either. My uncle also owned a garage and helped Kyle out of trouble at times. If the car got dented when he rolled it in a ditch, my uncle would fix it before I ever knew it was damaged. It was their secret because they both knew how upset I would have been, had I found out about it. I just couldn't figure out why his car always looked so dirty and scratched up. He had me really fooled. I thought he just didn't really care about his car or didn't try to keep it in good shape. Here all along, he was fooling around with another friend named Joel, who loved to speed down the country road that he lived on. Fortunately, they were never caught speeding. I really think Kyle thought that he was invincible at times. I remember talking to him several times about being safe and being cautious because I was always worried about him. I know it is in my nature as a mother to worry, but I think I worried more than most mothers' do. If I heard an ambulance siren, I always worried that it might be for one of my children, but Kyle would always smile at me and assure me that he was in God's hands and nothing was ever going to happen to him. Somehow, I told myself that God was going to take care of Kyle and he would be safe because God had already taken my father away from me, and he certainly wouldn't take my son too. I kept reassuring myself of this explanation, because I figured that God knew that I was already hurt enough.

Another one of his vehicle mishaps took place on the night of one of their high school concerts. He and another friend named Joseph decided that they would take a little ride in Joseph's new Jeep before the concert. They were already dressed up in their tuxedos for the concert, but it was early enough to take a few back roads on the way to the high school. Joseph wanted to show Kyle just what his new truck could do off-road. The only problem was that neither of them thought enough about how the fields and terrain would be after the heavy rain the night before. Needless to say, they got stuck in a huge muddy field! Joseph was sure that he could get the truck out because it had four-wheel drive, but the more and more he tried, the worse it became. They both looked at each other all dressed up in their tuxedos, and realized that they were in big trouble. Even though Joseph tried to laugh about it, Kyle began to be quite upset. He was never late for a performance or ever in trouble with his choir director, Mr. Tayne, and he didn't want to start that now. Kyle had the greatest respect for his teacher and felt that Mr. Tayne was like a father figure to him at times. Kyle spent many an afternoon talking with him, even at his home in his back yard among the hyacinths. Mr. Tayne loved gardening as well as music, and had an extensive collection of varieties of hyacinths. Kyle could relate to him about flowers too, after working in the greenhouse when he was younger.

But now, the two of them had to figure a way out of this mess that they had driven into. One of them would have to get out and give the truck a little push while the other one gave it the gas. It was the only way. Kyle volunteered to do the dirty work. When he got out, he thought he would try to look for some leaves and twigs to put under one of the tires for traction, but when he stepped out of the vehicle, his shoes actually got stuck in the mud! It was all he could do to keep his composure and not start laughing like his friend. Poor Kyle was so angry that he wanted to scream, but at the same time he couldn't keep a straight face any longer; so he laughed as well, until the tears rolled down his red cheeks. This just made Joseph laugh even harder, but they had to do something fast, or they would not make it to their concert on time. So Kyle carefully slipped out of his shoes and socks and rolled up his pant legs and went to the back of the truck barefoot, with the little leaves and twigs that he found around the area. Joseph applied the gas as Kyle pushed from behind, but the mud went flying! Poor Kyle was splashed from head to toe, but the truck finally made it out of the muck and mud. The only way to clean up their mess was the car wash, so they made a quick stop there and washed off the mud as best they could off of the truck and Kyle's tuxedo with the sprayer. Even though his pants were soaking wet then, at least they didn't look muddy and dirty; and hopefully by the time they got to the school, they wouldn't look as wet.

So with time running out, they quickly drove back to the highway, and made their way to the high school before the concert started. All the way there, Kyle was grumbling at Joseph about the whole incident. He frantically tried to get himself cleaned up and his tuxedo dried off, but unfortunately, he still looked drenched. When Mr. Tayne saw Kyle's clothes, he was very angry with him, but there wasn't any time for a reprimand then, because the concert was just about to begin. The two of them knew that they would be severely dealt with after the performance. Even though Joseph laughed every time he talked about it later on, Kyle never let him forget about the reprimand they got from Mr. Tayne after the concert.

Kyle was not used to being scolded by his favorite teacher and he didn't want to ruin his relationship with him. I also think that Mr. Tayne realized it was not Kyle that caused the situation, so he actually got off pretty easily. Once again Kyle's charming personality helped him out of a pretty bad situation.

Kyle in his tuxedo for a choir concert

Chapter Five

Searching

Before the Christmas of the year my mother died, Christmas was the best time of the year for our family. After she was gone, Christmas took on a little different meaning for all of us. One thing though, was the traditions that our mother started with us when we were kids, still remained in our celebrations year after year. I guess it is a way that all of us keep her memory alive. Even though she died three days before Christmas, and she was in very poor health, it didn't stop her from preparing for the Christmas festivities. She had her big tree up and decorated and she had all her presents bought, wrapped, and placed under it. The mantle of the fireplace was decorated with the Nativity scene on one side, and another little town setting on the other side. It reminded me of the houses in the story *A Christmas Carol*, complete with cotton batting to look like snow all around it. The Italian sausage was already purchased, the homemade bread was baked, and the cannoli shells were ready to be filled with our favorite ricotta and cornstarch pudding. She was ready for the family gathering on Christmas Eve at her little home, which she felt was as big as a beautiful mansion.

It was our tradition that all of the family would gather at Mama's on Christmas Eve for Italian sausage sandwiches, sautéed in wine with green peppers and onions. We always had lasagna, salad, wine, cannoli and cookies for dessert. Mama would have her girls gather with her to make her cuchidata or fig-filled cookies, and s and o cookies, frosted or rolled in sesame seeds, the week before Christmas. So on Christmas Eve, we would go early to midnight mass so that we could get a good seat, and then afterwards, we would have our little feast at Mama's, open presents, and party till the wee hours of the morning. This was and still is our family's Christmas tradition. The only difference is now, we gather at one of my sisters' homes each year, and we all bring one of the traditional holiday items to the party with us. But each and every year it seems to lose a little bit of the joy we once had when she was alive. However, we will always remember the laughter and fun that she brought to the festivities. She was the life of the party.

These were the memories that I kept in my heart each and every year that I prepared for the Christmas season at my little house with Kyle and Katerina. One beautiful Christmas comes to mind. It was a Christmas when the children were still very young. We hadn't been in our little house very long, so I felt that I had to do something to make that Christmas a memorable one where we would feel a little more secure and happy. I thought a nice big fancy Christmas tree would help to do that, so I found a good-sized tree at a garage sale that still looked like it was in decent shape. All I had to do was get some lights and ornaments to decorate it. My sister Giada worked at a fancy department store at that time, and the store decorators were giving away the old ornaments to the employees at cost. Giada bought several boxes of them for me because she knew I could use them. They were glass ornaments and they were all a faded pink color that looked like mauve or antique peach. I thought they looked great and I was delighted to have them. I put a few sets of white twinkle lights on the tree and I made bows out of a package of mauve pink-colored tissue paper. I also had a bit of pink flowered wallpaper left over from my bedroom project, so I cut it up and made a lot of tiny paper fans. I attached little pink ribbons to them and tied the fans on the tree. It turned out so beautiful, that when my friends and family members came over, they were amazed at the sight. It really looked expensive, but in reality, it was only about twenty dollars for all the decorations and the tree together. The only problem

I had with it was the tree stand. It was cracked and glued back together, so I had a little trouble keeping the tree straight. But with the help of a little rope tied around the upper half of the tree from one window latch to the other, it stood there quite straight. I just tucked the rope in and under the branches very carefully so that it was out of sight. It looked great when it was done, and it helped to brighten our Christmas spirit that year.

Many years later, when Kyle and Katerina were seniors in high school, another memory of Christmas comes back to me. Of course, our tree was decorated with many expensive glass and painted ornaments and little angels that I collected throughout the years. I especially liked the angels that glowed in the dark when the lights were turned off at night. There was also a little ballerina ornament that I bought Katerina after we went to see *The Nutcracker* one winter. It was a beautiful tree full of delightful decorations that brought back many happy memories. That year, I had everyone over to our home for the Christmas Eve celebration, so I was in charge of making the homemade bread and the Italian sausage. I always made the filling for the cannoli too, because my family liked that I added a bit of chopped maraschino cherries, a touch of cinnamon, and shaved chocolate to the filling. I decorated them with slivered almonds and powdered sugar after they were filled. So because of all the last-minute preparations I had to do, I went to an earlier mass that year by myself. Kyle and Katerina decided to go to midnight mass with their friends. They both arranged for their dates to meet them at our home, and then they went off to mass as a group. Katerina had her boyfriend Doug with her, and Kyle took his girlfriend, Jane. The four of them looked so nice that I took a few pictures of them together before they left.

It was a happy time for them, but after they left for mass, I sat down and thought about how far we had come together as our little family and how great my children turned out, especially since I really raised them all by myself. I was very proud of them, but at the same time, a tear came to my eye. Holidays were hard for me—especially because I was alone and had no companion of my own. Oh, I could have had a special someone if I wanted to, but one night back when Kyle was ten or eleven, a horrible thing happened to me, and because of it, I vowed never to have a man in my life again.

It was the evening that Kyle really did save my life. Because of some foolish actions on my part, I got myself into some serious trouble. I didn't realize it until it was almost too late. It seemed as if there wasn't any way out for me either, until that night when I was assaulted and almost went through the upstairs bedroom window. But because of Kyle's quick thinking and his call to 911, I was rescued just in time. Even though it was a very cold night in February, he stood outside on the front porch with the light on, and motioned for the police to come in and go directly upstairs to help. Kyle was my little hero that night.

From that moment on, it was apparent to me that Kyle was going to be my strength and protect me from harm. He had grown from a boy to man that night. He told me not to worry and that he would take care of me always. I just smiled at him and hugged him. Kyle was going to be the only male figure in our home that I needed around me now. It seemed that he had a special strength within him—a spiritual strength that changed him and helped him grow. As he went on through his high school years, this spiritual strength carried him through many experiences. He made a commitment to God that he would relay His word to everyone, in most everything that he did.

The friends that he hung around with at school also had to be spiritually alive, or he would preach to them and discuss their beliefs, until they became committed to their religious beliefs as well. Even if they were not Catholic beliefs, all of Kyle's friends had to believe in God and be able to discuss their faith with him—or he wouldn't consider them friends. Religion was always the most important thing in life to him. While in high school, Kyle joined the choir at our church. Even though he was the youngest adult singer that had ever tried out for the choir, his performance was so good that they had to let him in. He also was the most mature high school student that they had ever seen. Kyle loved to sing and it showed in his smile and in his twinkling eyes as he sang. Of course, when Latin was used in a song, Kyle smiled even more. He was always encouraging the organist and choir director to choose songs that were madrigals or psalms that could be sung. He loved religious music, medieval and baroque arias, or Gregorian chants. But if the music that was chosen was modern, Kyle would always grumble. I would hear him complain about it over and over, until they were through performing that type of music or that song. I just chuckled to myself about how old-fashioned and different his thinking was.

Kyle also devoted his time, outside of school, to teaching religious education at our church to the children that did not go to the parochial school. Again, he had to prove to the priest that he knew enough about religion and Catholicism to be able to teach the students, even though he was only a high school student himself. The first year, he taught the fifth-grade religion class, and the following year, he taught the second-grade students, before they made their First Communion. It was an honor to Kyle, because that was a very important time in a child's religious education. The students had to be properly prepared for the sacrament of the Eucharist, and Kyle made sure they were.

His performance in his senior year play was also related to his religious beliefs. I don't know if Kyle had encouraged the teacher to pick this play or not, but it was decided that the school would perform *The Lion, the Witch, and the Wardrobe* that year. Kyle tried out, and won the part of Aslan, the lion. He was so thrilled and I was so proud of him. He was going to be the main star of the play, and he was suited for the part more than anyone else at the school.

The play was an inspiration from the book written by C.S. Lewis from his collection called *The Chronicles of Narnia*. It borrows ideas from religion, and illustrates basic concepts of Christianity. Some of the characters in it are synonymous with biblical figures. It is an allegory of Christ's crucifixion, and Aslan is the Christ-like figure that is humiliated, persecuted, executed at the stone table, and resurrected at the end of the play. Aslan sacrifices himself to release the child who betrayed them from the spell of the White Witch. From his sacrifice, all the children were freed from the Land of Narnia, as Aslan is resurrected.

For many weeks, Kyle was so excited about performing in this play as he studied his lines. You could see that he would relate his performance to his religious beliefs and do his best to play the part of Aslan. His only worry was the costume itself. The school rented an actual lion costume, but it was made for a person that was shorter in stature than Kyle, and lighter in weight. He was poured into it and he always worried that he would rip the costume if he took a deep breath or tried to actually stand up straight. But his heart was filled with his desire to do the best performance that he could do, and he pulled it off with only a slight tear in the costume. It was repaired before it was returned without an extra fee.

The best part for me was watching Kyle, of course. I went to every performance, either with Giada and Leonardo, Katerina, or all by myself. I had to see it every time, and again, after each performance, my heart was filled with motherly love and pride for my son's achievements. So many people stopped me, after each performance, to let me know how much they enjoyed the play and how much spirit Kyle brought to his part in it as Aslan. Even weeks later, I would hear comments about Kyle from phone calls, or chance meetings while shopping, from friends and family that saw him in the play. The thing that I heard the most was how well Kyle was suited for the part. Everyone said with a chuckle, that it was right up his alley. My sister and I agreed.

After his last high school play was over, and the extra work and excitement had passed, Kyle settled back into his rudimentary life of work and school. Katerina had her friends that were in volleyball and basketball. She was more interested in sports, even though she still sang in the women's choir, just to keep Kyle happy.

Kyle & Katerina at their high school graduation

After they graduated from high school, I was fortunate enough to be qualified to get both of them full-paid grants for college from the government, because of my low income. Their grades were good enough to be accepted, Katerina being an average student, and Kyle with above-average grades, and scholastic achievements in music. He could have had all A's if he would have only applied himself a little more, but he didn't. He only worked real hard at a subject if he was really interested in it. But at least they both were given the chance to try out college. They both enrolled in the community college in our city. At first, they took all the required subjects, just as their advisors had planned. But going to lecture classes, taking notes, studying, and doing homework all over again dragged them down. They both came to the conclusion that college wasn't going to be fun. There was no time for socialization. This was much more than they had expected it to be, and unfortunately, the two of them gave up and dropped out. I was disappointed with them, but I couldn't force them to continue with school. They were convinced that college was not their cup of tea. They both were going to look for a profession in areas that didn't require a college degree.

Even though we all say, at one time or another, that we hate change, it can be a refreshing thing in one's life when the decision to make that change is your own. After several years working in the paint department, Kyle felt that he needed a change. He told me that he put in a request for a transfer at his work. He knew he could get a management position if he transferred. I remember hearing him say that his best friend, Sam, transferred to another store location, and I think that influenced Kyle to do the same. He would make a lot more money at another location. This store was in a much bigger city than ours, and it would take him about thirty minutes longer to drive there for work. That would be a big change in itself for Kyle, since all of the jobs that he had so far were only five minutes away from home. But Kyle missed his friend Sam so much that he decided to follow him and also make the big move. Things just weren't as much fun at our town's store without Sam around and the excitement that Kyle saw from Sam's undercover work. So Kyle's transfer was approved and he started work in the big city the following week.

Because of the distance he would have to go, Kyle knew that he would need a better vehicle—especially during the winter months. He decided to look for a truck because he would feel much safer in a small pickup, instead of his little two-door sedan. So, on the way home from work that day, he stopped at the used car lot to look around. Right away, he spied a little, dark green Sonoma pickup, and he made up his mind to buy it. He took me over there to look at it that same day, and get my opinion on his decision. It looked great on the outside, as if it was well cared for, but it had over 100,000 miles on it. I really didn't think it was worth the money, or that the engine would last very long, considering the miles it had, but I couldn't change Kyle's mind about buying it. He had a stubborn streak in him, and there was no way I could convince him to still look around. I figured that at least we could count on my uncle who owned the garage to help us fix it if something went wrong. So, within that same week, he was driving around in his little green pickup and showing it off to all his friends.

It made it through the winter months that year, but by the spring, the transmission was slipping and needed to be replaced. Of course, Kyle had such a high payment schedule on that little green truck that he couldn't afford to fix the transmission without help from my sister Giada's husband, Leonardo. Good old Unc, as Kyle would call him, came to the rescue, and bailed him out. He loaned Kyle the money to purchase a refurbished transmission from my uncle, and fix the truck. Leonardo set up a payment schedule for Kyle to pay back his loan to him with minimal interest and economical payments. He trusted Kyle to pay him back, little by little, because he would not have been able to afford another bank loan for the repairs. This would be just the beginning of Kyle's financial troubles that eventually would wear him down, practically to the breaking point.

The adjustment to the new job started off all right, but quickly became unsettling to Kyle. He was told that he would be managing a much larger paint department there, but after a few weeks, he realized that he might have made a big mistake by moving. It seemed that there were other guys in the same department that were also told that they would be the manager on their shift; but at some of those shift assignments, the same guys had to work together. This caused a lot of friction between Kyle and some of the other guys that he worked with. They seemed at times to have a power struggle going on between them. The store's undercover procedures were also very different, and Sam was never around to talk to Kyle. At times, I could see the sadness on his face when he would come home from work, and I think it really dragged him down. The only good thing about this move to Kyle was the friendships that he developed with several of the girls he met that also worked there. He started dating a couple of girls on a regular basis.

He even brought one girl home to meet me. I could see by the look on their faces when I met her, that they were serious about each other.

She was a very soft-spoken, petite girl, with delicate features and a very kind personality. I could tell by the conversation I had with her at dinner that she was quite intelligent and career-minded. She had almost finished working on her master's degree in psychology at the university when I met her. We engaged in the most delightful conversations about teaching, child development, religion, and music. I liked her from the moment I met her, and I couldn't wait to really sit down and have a heart-to-heart talk with Kyle about his plans with her for the future. I was sure that this would be the girl that he would want to settle down with. She had all the qualities that he was looking for, from what he told me. But after dating her for a few months, he changed his mind. Kyle was so concerned that she might be harboring some deep-hidden secrets and some psychological problems from her past that she was dealing with. He was afraid that this was something that she was hiding from him, and it just made him want to run away from her. He stopped seeing her abruptly then, and really didn't explain his reasons for doing so to her. I couldn't understand how or why he did that, but I guess there are just some things that a mother never really can figure out about her son. It seems that as a son grows up, he also grows further and further away from his mother, when it comes to expressing his innermost feelings to her. It must have something to do with being a man and not showing emotions anymore—especially to a man's mother. All I know is that it saddened me and shattered my hopes and dreams for his future.

Then along came another girlfriend. Now this girl was quite the opposite of the first one—who was pure, refined, quiet, and delicate. This girl was not shy, but outspoken, and fashionably dressed. She seemed to me to be exactly the opposite of the first girl he met there. I was uncomfortable meeting her at first, but eventually, I learned from Kyle that she really was a very wonderful girl. She was a lot more outgoing and a lot more fun to be with, as far as Kyle was concerned. But as long as Kyle was happy being with her, then I was happy for him too. I had to learn not to ask too many questions and not to meddle in his affairs, or I would lose the communication and trust that I gained with my son. Kyle was always open and honest with me, and told me everything up until then, but when it came to his girlfriends now, he was quiet. He never brought another girl home to meet me after that, and I never heard any more about her or any other girl from then on.

At the same time that Kyle was having difficulty working with some of the guys in his department, Sam was having problems as well. It seemed to both of them that it had to be the fault of the management at that location. Sam was just as disappointed with his position as Kyle was, and so he decided he needed a change in jobs as well. But this time, the two of them would be going in different directions. Sam started looking around and landed a job as the chief managing security officer for a chain of pizza stores in the downriver area. This was his dream job and he knew it was going to work out fine for him. He would be traveling to each store after it closed for the evening, and check the security cameras and install fresh film for the cameras to record.

When Kyle realized that Sam made another change that worked out well, Kyle thought about what he could do in his life to better himself. He never really enjoyed working in retail anyway, because sometimes he just had such a struggle trying to please certain customers.

"It was those darned women," as he would say, "that demanded that their custom-mixed paint match the exact color of their living room couch!" that upset him the most.

To him, women like that were very difficult to please. So Kyle decided that he would find some kind of work outside where he could be in the open air and feel the breeze on his face. He remembered that his grandfather on his dad's side really enjoyed working on the railroad, and he made a good living as an engineer for a steel company downriver. Kyle looked up to his grandfather and enjoyed hearing the stories he told about working on the trains when he was alive. So that was where he started to look for work. Luckily, he was able to land a job at a small railroad switching company downriver that loaded automobiles for transport. The pay was just a bit more than he was making at the department store, but he felt so free being able to work outside, even if it was in the cold.

Kyle and Sam still maintained their close friendship. They would get together at least a couple times a week and talk about religion and their jobs and family gatherings. When Kyle was off for a couple of days, Sam would take him along on his security checks at a few downtown locations. It gave them time to talk and reminisce as well. Kyle also enjoyed the nightlife at our home with Sam and his girlfriend, Jan. When I would make Kyle a batch of homemade bread, he would be sure to let Sam and Jan know when it was going to be ready. The three of them would quietly sneak in after I went to bed, and have a little wine- and bread-tasting party while they played cards. Kyle always encouraged me to make at least seven loaves of bread each week. He told me that the seven loaves were for the seven tribes of Israel. I never really understood that, because I read in the Bible that there were twelve tribes of Israel, but later I found out that he was talking about the tribes before they received their inheritance from God. He always had some comment to make that related to the Bible—one way or another. That was his unique personality coming out. Making all that bread was a lot of work, but it made him happy, so I couldn't disappoint him. I always knew though, when Sam and Jan had visited, because there were several loaves of bread missing the next morning! That was okay though, because I heard from Kyle the next morning about how much they enjoyed dipping it in olive oil and asiagio cheese. When he said things like that, it always made me feel pretty good.

When Kyle wasn't working or goofing around with Sam, he would be cooking up some extravagant scheme to make some extra money—and it usually would involve Ned somehow. Even though Ned meant well, he couldn't stop Kyle from over-indulging and getting out of control when it came to spending his money. The internet was the easiest way that Kyle was able to do this. When he was home, I could always find him upstairs on the computer. Instead of buying or selling uniform hats or medals online, like he did when he was younger, he was buying and selling Bibles and other religious books with his own money now, so I couldn't say anything about it. He even convinced Katerina to take a long drive with him to the antique malls and villages around to look for Bibles and other religious books. After several months though, he developed a pretty extensive collection of religious books in his room, and it was his goal to study and read them all. He wanted to be prepared to discuss any form of religion with anyone he talked to. That seemed to be his main purpose in life. The only problem that I had with all of it was the phone bill that he ran up for me. Even though he was very generous with his money when it came to his friends and helping them out, it was like pulling teeth for me to get any money from him for the phone bill. Finally, I had to have my long-distance service cut off because I couldn't afford to pay the outrageous bills he caused me. I even had to put a special code on the line, which also cost an extra fee, just to stop him from calling long distance at all. I had to be tough on him sometimes, because he still kept trying to step over that line with me. Sometimes, tough love was the only thing that worked on Kyle. He was simply not able to control his spending without it.

Kyle also schemed in other ways. When his dream of the seminary in our area didn't work out, he still didn't give up entirely. He was constantly searching. I eventually found out that he contacted the Jesuit priests in a few other states south of us. He also wrote to the Josephinium Seminary near my sister Tina's home in Ohio, and requested information for study there. He was still searching, even though he liked his job on the railroad. In reality, I think he really didn't want to give up on the priesthood. The way I found out about that was from Tina herself. She told me that one afternoon, she heard a knock on her back door, and was surprised by an unexpected visit from Kyle. He went down there to visit the Josephinium Seminary, and stopped by to see her as well. After talking for a while with her and my brother-in-law, Todd, he confronted them with his scheme. Kyle thought that he would be able to afford to go to the Josephinium, if it would be possible to live with my sister while he studied there. That would save him a lot of money—enough to be able to pay for his tuition on his own. I felt badly for him because I could see that he was becoming desperate, but Tina was overwhelmed at the thought of having to cook for Kyle. He was such a big eater, and then also, she would have had to clean up after him as well, and do his laundry. It was simply way too much work for her to attempt to do. Her health was just too frail because of her rheumatic heart. She really felt bad to tell him no, but it simply would not work. So again, Kyle searched for happiness in a job or a career that would make his life feel fulfilled.

Besides working on the trains, Kyle had a soft place in his heart for tractors. When he was very little, his grandfather sat him on his lap as he rode one of his tractors around in the fields between our houses. Grandpa was a collector of tractors. That was his hobby. He had more tractors in his yard than he had acres of property! He would just line them up in the yard as if they were on display. The funny thing was that Grandpa really wasn't much of a mechanic and most of the tractors didn't run very well. It was his grandmother that actually was the mechanic in the family. She was very good at taking small engines apart and repairing them. She also loved to work on sewing machines and old phones. That was her hobby. So together, they had quite a collection of tractors, lawn mowers, sewing machines, and other small mechanical devices out on the lawn and all through their house. The two of them must have had a lot of influence on Kyle though, because when he was in his early twenties, he made tractor collecting his hobby also, even though we lived in the city. I think it started when he was younger and he took our lawn mower apart to see how the engine parts went together. My neighbor had to come to his rescue and help him put the thing back together. We all laughed and scolded him saying, "You don't fix what isn't broken!"

I think being able to put it back together, finally, gave him the bug to work on other engines. He used the internet to find old tractors that he could buy, restore, and then sell for a profit. He even bought several lawn mowers and a roto-tiller that was returned to the store. He still had his connection of friends there that would let him know when something good was returned. It could be purchased again at a great price because of a dent or a scratch on it. If it was something that wasn't running right, he figured he could take it apart, get it working properly, and then sell it on his own. My garage was becoming a small engine repair shop! My neighbors chuckled when they saw Kyle in our back yard, in the city, riding around on a tractor! He would even take one out for a spin around the streets in our neighborhood to make sure it was running right. I was amazed that the city police didn't give him too much trouble about it either. I think that when they stopped him and talked to him about his hobby, they also were quite impressed with his tractor restoration. It really was an unusual hobby for a young man, but I was glad that he wasn't buying motorcycles or fast cars instead. The only thing that bothered me was what his tractors did to my back yard. He insisted on leveling the area back by the garage so he would have more room to ride his tractors around. I had several beautiful fruit trees back there and a fig tree that my grandfather planted, but Kyle managed to destroy them all with his tractors and the roto-tiller. He used the tiller to work up the ground and then replant the area with new grass seed. He wasn't satisfied until the whole area was flattened. Little by little, he cleared the back yard, removed the fig tree and the other fruit trees, and covered the area with more soil so that he could plant more grass seed. He replanted the seed three times before I finally blocked the area off so that the lawn could regrow!

He would laugh and say, "I have to go farm the back forty," which was forty feet—not forty acres. That was his excuse to keep redoing the lawn. He was so proud of himself though, when he actually got one of his old tractors to put-put and purr like a kitten. His face would be beaming with a huge smile and a twinkle in his eye.

Kyle's favorite antique tractor that he restored

Tractors really did make him happy. He managed to buy and sell a few tractors and equipment, but the loans that he took out to buy them had financially overburdened him; and he spent way too much money trying to restore most of them. Eventually, he had to ask good old Unc again, to help him out of another mess. Leonardo really did try hard to teach Kyle how to manage his money. He set up another agreement with Kyle on the repayment schedule and had Kyle sign it and promise to make regular payments on the loans he took out with him. It would work for a while, and then Kyle would miss a payment and I would have to bug him about it. I didn't want to cause any hard feelings between my sister and me over money, so I held him to his promise to repay his debts. I guess that is why Kyle started looking for another railroad job that would give him more income. Every time that he read about a hiring session at a railroad company, he would go to it—even if he had to miss a day of work. These hiring sessions would take all day, if he passed the written test with a high score. Each group would be eliminated eventually, little by little, until there were only a dozen candidates left waiting for an interview. At most of the sessions that he went to, he made it through to the last group of guys that were qualified for the positions. The trouble was that there would be only a couple of openings that all of them were applying for, and he would just miss being hired next. It was very frustrating for Kyle because he dreamed of being a conductor or a switchman for a major railroad company. He would never give up on his dream.

Chapter Six

Traveling

After more than ten years of hard work at the greenhouse, I finally had achieved enough good graces with my employer to be rewarded with vacation days. I actually would be able to take a whole week off and be paid for it! I was ecstatic at the thought of going somewhere, but then I thought about vacation costs and spending money that in reality should be used for bills. It was futile. I could go somewhere, anywhere, but there was no way I would be able to afford it, even with the time off and the week's pay. When my sister Giada heard of my dilemma, like a saint, she came to my rescue. Her husband, Leonardo, was tired of going on trips with her all over the world, since they already went on twenty different vacations on almost every continent in the world. So, he suggested that she take me along with her on her next vacation, and she agreed that would be a wonderful idea. So that summer, she arranged a trip to Ireland for the two of us. Not only did she pay for the plane fare and the lodgings, but she even included a generous amount of spending money for me as well. That way I had no expenses to worry about and my paid time off at work could be used at home for bills and groceries for the kids while I was gone. I would have nothing to worry about except the kids themselves. The only thing I thought was that the kids might have a party or two while I was gone, so I threatened them with my neighbor's watchful eyes. The kids knew that Gramma Z would keep a close watch on them and make sure that they wouldn't get into any trouble while I was gone. So I gratefully accepted her invitation and let the kids know about my trip. I really wasn't worried about leaving them home alone. They certainly were old enough, at eighteen and nineteen, but were they responsible enough to stay alone, take care of the dogs, and still keep the house standing? I had to trust them. It was hard for me, but I knew they were capable and mature. The only thing that I thought they would probably pull, of course, would be drinking at their party while I was gone. That was inevitable. I just hoped that they would stay in control, and not let their friends drive drunk. So the plans were set and on the following Thursday, Kyle, Katerina, and Leonardo took us to the airport, and we were on our way to Ireland.

The ten-day guided tour was a whirlwind course on the history, beauty, and culture of the Emerald Isle. We were on the go every day from 6:00 a.m. until 9:00 p.m. traveling from Dublin, through the Ring of Kerry, and Cork, through Galway, and ending in Limerick. My most treasured memories were of the lush beauty of this tropical island, the culture, the lovely people we met, and of course, the churches that we visited. But above all, I will never forget standing on the spot where St. Patrick converted the king of Ireland to Christianity and seeing the monument of the Celtic cross that marked that spot. I wrote a daily journal of all our excursions. Also, I took notes on all the comments about the history and culture of the country from our tour guide. I think I used about twenty rolls of film because I wanted to take a picture of everything I saw. Every church I went into drew me closer to the Lord, and renewed my Catholic faith. I made sure to bring home a Celtic cross for Kyle and a St. Brigid's cross for Katerina. I also picked up any religious material I could find from all the churches I visited. Katerina's only other request was a silver ring, which I purchased for her in Cork. It was a remarkable journey for me, and to this day, I can still remember Ireland and all its beauty. I was truly spoiled by my sister, and will be forever grateful to her for her generosity.

When I returned home, I was very pleased and proud of my children. The neighbors told me that they did have a party, but it was very quiet and did not get out of control. The house was still standing and everything seemed to be in order, as if I had never left. I almost felt let down, as if something terrible should have happened. It was hard to believe that nothing bad did happen. I guess the kids had truly grown up in spite of my doubts.

So, when the next summer vacation was planned, it was easier to agree to go again with Giada to Europe. This time, she planned a trip that went from England, to Switzerland, to Belgium, to Luxembourg, and finally to France. She paid for everything again and also gave me more than enough spending money, and money to buy presents for the kids as well. This also was a ten-day trip, and another guided, whirlwind of a tour! Again, I wrote a daily journal, and took plenty of pictures.

I have to say that the churches were what impressed me the most, and I made sure to bring home every piece of religious material that I could find for Kyle. The only souvenir that he requested was a Bible from France. I couldn't find one small enough to carry back, so I bought him a rosary from a little store next to the Notre Dam Cathedral. Katerina wanted another silver ring. London and Paris were the most memorable and exciting cities for me, but I will never forget the Louvre, the Notre Dam Cathedral and the Rose window. The best site of all was the Church of the Sacre Coeur on top of Monte Martre in Paris. When I went inside, my heart was filled with the beauty and the warmth of the entire church, which was lit by wooden candelabra throughout. I knelt down there and prayed silently and thanked God for all the gifts that he had given me and to be able to travel and see the beauty of Europe. I also remember standing in the square in front of the Notre Dam Cathedral, on that special spot, and making a wish to return to Paris some day. It still is one of my dreams.

Upon our return home again, the kids made me proud. Nothing was damaged and there were no complaints from the neighbors. The only thing they did that was hard for me to deal with was the change they made in the setup of the living room furniture. When I walked in the door, everything was in a different place, and of course for me, change is hard to do. But after a while, I got used to it, and it became a refreshing move for me.

The final European tour that Giada planned and paid for again the following year was to Italy. I guess she wanted to save the best for last. It truly was the best for me. My fiftieth birthday was approaching, and the days on the tour worked out perfectly for me. I turned fifty on the last night of our tour, and at that last night, we happened to be back in Rome. The whole group celebrated my fiftieth birthday with a special little cake for me at our farewell dinner. That truly was a very memorable moment for me. But it didn't overshadow all the beauty of Rome and the hillside towns and cathedrals we traveled to. We went from one side of Italy through many hill towns, to Florence, Assisi, Venice, and back to Rome and the Vatican City. I prayed in every church, and bought Kyle and Katerina a rosary at the Vatican. I am very proud to say that I have been in the Vatican museum and especially proud to say that I have seen the ceiling in the Sistine Chapel. Of course, to be able to enter into many of the most famous cathedrals in Italy was truly remarkable, but the most impressive one for me, besides St. Peter's Basilica, was the cathedral in the little hill town of Orvieto in the region of Umbria. It is the Gothic Cathedral of St. Andrea, which has frescos that date from 1499. It was there that the miracle of Bolsena occurred during a mass in the Chapel of San Britico. The Communion host dripped blood onto the altar cloth, which is now encased in glass in the chapel along with the highest peak of the façade of the cathedral. I truly have been blessed to have been in that cathedral and been given the opportunity to see many other cathedrals and churches in Italy. I just kept thinking of how I wished that Kyle could have seen it all with me.

When I returned from this trip, the furniture had not been moved, and they didn't even have a party with their friends. I was surprised though, when I went down to the basement the next day to do my laundry. They spent several days cleaning it up! The basement looked great! The only problem was that when Kyle decided to clean the basement, he threw away everything that wasn't nailed down! All the chairs and other small items of furniture that were downstairs were thrown out to the trash. He also threw away all the extra clothes of mine that I had stored down there! I was not very happy about that, but the deed was done.

After being treated to the awesome beauty of Europe on three wonderful vacations, I told Giada that I was really feeling guilty, and that I could never repay her for her generosity toward me. She didn't expect any repayment, although she really spoiled me. I decided that I just couldn't go on any more trips to Europe with her. I saw so much, and she spent too much money on me already. So she agreed that she would only pay for the plane fare for me to go down to visit her and Leonardo in Florida during the winter months. I would stay with them for just a week, and they could show me the sights in Florida and do a little shopping. It would be a nice treat to go swimming and lie in the warm sun during our cold February climate here. So right before Valentine's Day here, I flew down to Florida for my next year's vacation. It was like going to Tahiti or Hawaii for me. The sun and the sandy beaches were beautiful! Their Florida home was only twelve miles from the gulf coast and the sand was white and smooth, and sparkled like glitter in the sun. It was a nice relaxing getaway, compared to the structure of the guided tours we took in Europe. I was very comfortable there, and happy, until I got back home.

Kyle was still having financial troubles and couldn't seem to curb his spending, or keep on top of his bills. Even though Leonardo helped him out twice financially, he was still deep in debt, though he didn't tell anyone about it. I didn't notice any furniture rearranged or any of my articles of clothing missing this time. The furniture hadn't changed, but yet I just felt that something was wrong. He seemed very tense and a little distant toward me. I asked Katerina what went on while I was gone, but she felt that nothing unusual really happened. She was so busy with her own work and social life that she didn't see much of Kyle either.

If he wasn't working, he was out somewhere with one of his friends, and of course, I had no clue. He wouldn't tell me who he was with, or where he was going, or when he would return. He felt he was too old now to report in to his mother, and I couldn't argue about that anymore either. I just had to trust him and keep my worries to myself. I didn't really know what shift he was working on now either, because working on the railroad could mean any time of the day or night. So when he came home in the middle of the night, I had no idea where he had been.

After about a week of being home and back to work, when I was organizing papers and bills on the desk in the kitchen, I noticed a few receipts and a bit of change that Kyle must have left there when he emptied out his pockets. Among the receipts, I found one from a restaurant and one from a department store. But then I found one from the pawnshop downtown. I thought that was unusual for Kyle. Why would he be going to a pawnshop? Was he buying jewelry, or was he selling something? My curiosity was aroused, and so I decided to do what a mother really shouldn't ever do, but I was worried. So I started going through his personal items and drawers in his room. First, I looked in his jewelry box where he kept his cuff links and watches and rings. I was not surprised to find that most of his rings were missing. The one that Giada gave him with the red stone was gone. The one that I gave him that was my father's initial ring wasn't there either. I also could see that a couple of his pocket watches were missing. He had at least five different ones that he showed me, and now there was only one in there. I knew that he always kept everything in that box, and now there were only a few items left. He must have been really hurting for money, or he wouldn't have sold his favorite treasures like that. Then I looked at his Bible collection, and I could see that several places on the shelves had empty spots where a book had been taken out. I didn't know which ones, but I knew they were missing because he never left any of them just lying around somewhere. They were always organized neatly on his bookcase. I felt badly for him. He must have been desperate to sell those special books. I also found paperwork from E-Bay on his desk while I was going through his things. That must have been how he was getting extra money. It all was making sense to me now.

The sad and sometimes intense look on his face, and the nervousness I could sense from him when he was near, were all a result from these transactions. What could I do to help him? I didn't have any extra money in the bank that I could give him, and he knew that, or he would have asked me for my help. I also couldn't tell him that I knew what was going on, or he would realize that I had gone through his things. All I could do was pray for him, and of course—worry. That was one thing I did best, and when I worried, I felt the need to start cleaning around the house. I started dusting in the living room, but when I got to the piano, my heart dropped. My bassoon and my flute were gone! I knew I didn't move them! They were always there, right next to the piano, along with my clarinet! I was the only one who played them, so I knew they were gone. I couldn't believe it. I didn't want to accuse Kyle, but how else could they have been missing? There was no way that someone could have stolen them. Why would someone come in and take just those two things anyway? I was so hurt. How could he do this to me? I knew I had to confront him now when he came home, but all I could do at that moment was sit down and cry. Those instruments were not just a hobby for me—they were part of my life, and my past as a music teacher. He must have taken them when I was in Florida. I knew they were there before I went, because I cleaned house a couple of days right before I left for Florida, and they weren't missing then. So I waited patiently for his return and thought calmly about how I would confront him. It made me nervous, but I had to remain calm and talk to him without losing my temper.

It would only be a few hours before he would be coming home from work, so I kept myself distracted as I continued to clean around the house. I had dinner cooking, and when he finally walked in the door, he went straight to the kitchen and started taste-testing the chicken soup I had simmering on the stove. It was one of his favorites. It would be easier to confront him about it while he was eating, so I simply and calmly asked him what happened to my flute and my bassoon. He turned around, and with a mouth full of bread dipped in the broth, mumbled to me in a surprised tone that he didn't know. I asked him again, because I knew that I had caught him. I could always tell by the look on his face when he was lying to me, and he knew it. This time his response to me was that I didn't play them anymore. He shrugged his shoulders and turned around as he grabbed another piece of bread and dipped it into the simmering pot. I turned around and walked away silently and thought about how upset I was with him. It would take me many months before I would be able to forgive him. This was the worst thing that he could have done to me, but I really think that he didn't even know how important those instruments were to me. For at least a week, I gave him the cold shoulder. I didn't want to talk to him at all. I simply avoided being around him. Other than talking to Katerina a little, I was silent. He never did apologize to me, but I knew in my heart that eventually he would be very, very sorry for what he did.

As soon as spring started showing its warmth and color in the flowerbeds, Kyle started working diligently on one of his tractors in the garage. Soon, he had it running, and except for touching up the original paint, he had the Farmall Cub ready for sale. He somehow managed to collect several attachments that also went with that particular tractor, so he decided to sell them all together. This would make it a much quicker sell. He must have had it advertised on E-Bay, because shortly after that, a man from Canada agreed on the price, and drove down with a trailer to pick it up. It was a good buy for the man, and Kyle made a sizable profit. I was happy for him, and hoped that the extra money would get him out of the bind that he was in. At least it would help him for a little while. He just wasn't making much money lately because he was working on call at the railroad, and that wasn't always a steady forty-hour week. Kyle still loved working on the railroad, but he just wanted to get a position with a class-one or class-two railroad, instead of the third-class railroad job that he had. Everyone that knew Kyle always chuckled when he talked about being a switchman/conductor and the work that it involved—coupling and uncoupling the cars, throwing the locking mechanisms, and climbing up and down those little ladders, on a slow-moving train. He would smile and his eyes would sparkle when he talked about it and how much he loved the work. It definitely was manual labor, and Kyle always told everyone that he wanted a job that didn't involve manual labor, and here he was doing it and loving it! We just couldn't understand him. Something about being on a railroad train must have surely changed his mind, because he was hooked on the railroad.

He continued working there, but he never stopped trying to better himself. Every time he heard of a hiring session, he would go, but he wouldn't get hired. Then one day, he heard of an opening in a railroad that was actually two hours from our home, but it was at a class-two railroad, so he thought he would apply for the job. He went for an interview there, and he was hired the next day! He was so excited. The job was going to start at a much higher pay level than he had at the time, but it was a bit of a drive. He thought that if it worked out for him, then he would move to that town to be closer to the job. But when he came home from the first day of work there, he was very troubled. The foreman on his shift told him that he had to clean out box cars instead of being a switchman like he thought he was hired for. He was also told that he was not allowed any breaks during his shift—not even a lunch break. He wasn't even allowed to take a bathroom break either. The foreman also said that he was also misinformed about the hourly pay. It was not anywhere near to what he was told from the man that hired him. It was a real sham, and if he stayed there, he would end up working for less money and driving a lot farther to get there. So the next morning, Kyle reluctantly called the supervisor that hired him and told him that it was just not going to work out. That afternoon, he drove back there and returned all the equipment and came home. He was broken, but not yet beaten. This search would go on for months, because he would never stop looking.

Another February came, and Giada asked me to come and visit her again in Florida. I was reluctant about going because I thought about what Kyle might do this time while I was gone. It would only be for one week, but after a talk with him, I was reassured that he wouldn't try anything like that again. So the next week I was on my way to Florida again. The first day, I didn't try to call home, but the second day I did. I just wanted to make sure everything was okay at home and Kyle wasn't doing anything wrong. The only problem was that I couldn't get him to answer the phone at all. I kept trying his cell phone and the home phone just about every hour, but I couldn't get through to him. I was frantic! What if he was in the hospital or something! I couldn't even get Katerina on her cell phone. I knew she was working a lot, but then again, when she wasn't working, she was with her boyfriend. It became very frustrating for me, and I worried so much about Kyle, that for three days, my vacation was totally ruined. All I could think about was that something terrible must have happened. On the fourth day, I finally got him on the phone, and he told me that he went to the Upper Peninsula looking for a job! That was why his cell phone didn't even work. They have very few towers in the area where he went. He had an interview at a railroad up there, but he realized that it was just not right for him. The area was so secluded, and the railroad yard there was even smaller than the one here, so he decided that it wouldn't work out. Even though it was unintentional on his part, Kyle ruined another vacation for me again.

It would be six more months before Kyle would actually see the light at the end of the tunnel. He was still using the computer to search for a better railroad job, and he finally was able to correspond with someone that returned his e-mail with a phone call. I just came home from work at noon, and he greeted me with a huge smile and a big hug. I knew something great had happened for him. He told me that the vice president of a large railroad company in Texas had returned his e-mail and called him about a job interview! He thought that he had been corresponding with the human resources department, but was actually talking to one of the owners! He asked Kyle to report the next morning for the interview! But it was a twenty-one-hour drive to Texas, and the only way he would be able to get there on time would be with the help of Katerina. She agreed to go with him and help him drive, even though she would have to take time off from her job. This had to be a quick decision, or he wouldn't make it there in time for the interview. That was how most large railroad companies worked. This man thought that it would be practically impossible for Kyle to make it there at such short notice, so Kyle would most likely decline the offer. He asked me what I thought about getting a job in Texas and moving, so I told him that he should do what would make him the happiest. If it meant moving to Texas, then I wouldn't stand in his way. Kyle knew that was what they would expect of him, so he accepted the offer for an interview at 10:00 the next morning. The two of them quickly packed a change of clothing, and were off in Katerina's little red truck. At least with her vehicle, I wouldn't worry as much, because it was newer and had fewer miles on it than Kyle's older green truck. They stopped at the gas station, filled it up, checked the oil and tires, bought some coffee, and were off to Houston. All I could do was say some prayers that God would keep them safe, and they would make it there on time.

Every four or five hours I called them if I hadn't heard from either of them. They planned to let one of them sleep for four hours, while the other one drove. That way, they could continue and still be alert enough to drive. The only problem was the caffeine. At times, it was hard to sleep if they had too much in their systems. Once Katerina called laughing hysterically, and told me that Kyle kept seeing a deer jump across the road in front of them. Of course, that made me worry even more, but all they could do was laugh, especially hearing the way Kyle would describe the deer and how they would just miss hitting it—over and over again! He had way too much caffeine in his system, and I was worried that he might have a heart attack from the elevated blood pressure that it caused. But things like that didn't even faze the two of them—they were invincible.

I had a terrible time trying to sleep that night through my worries, but by early the next morning, I was told that they had made it there safely. Kyle reported to his interview with just a few minutes to spare. He only had time to wash his face and quickly change his clothes before they found the right office. Kyle was lucky that he had a friend that lived in Houston, so he was able to direct them to the railroad yard over the cell phone. Through their drive down, Kyle explained the whole situation to him and so he agreed to let Kyle stay with him for a while, if he actually did get the job. During Kyle's interview, it was nice that Katerina would be able to visit with their friend and his family also.

After the interview, Kyle was sent directly to an outpatient medical facility to have a thorough examination. This was the standard procedure at that company, if someone was actually going to be hired. Kyle was uncertain, but very hopeful, that he might be hired. When I talked to him later that day, he told me that he thought the interview went very well. He was told that his persistence in seeking this position had a lot to do with the offer for an interview, especially after driving twenty-one hours to get there! Kyle told me later that he called there at least sixteen times to ask for an interview! The human resources director chuckled as he told Kyle that he was very curious to see what a young man like him looked like, after all the e-mails and phone calls that were made. I guess that his persistence paid off, because that afternoon, Kyle called me to tell me that if his physical checked out okay, he would start work there in two weeks! He was ready to make his big move to Texas.

After they stayed overnight, Katerina and Kyle were back on their way home for another twenty-one-hour drive. I was happy for him, but it would be bittersweet for me. When he moved away from home, I knew that I would lose Kyle forever. He probably would really like the job down there and he would find a nice girl and get married and start a family. I had to let go; after all, Katerina had already moved into an apartment in town, but she was still close to home. She was only ten minutes away if I needed her. I would always call her if she didn't call me, and we would see each other at least once a week. But when Kyle moved out, I would be alone. It was going to be hard for me—I just knew it, but I had to let go.

When the two of them got home and we told all the family the news, Giada and Donita decided to give Kyle a farewell party. There was just two weeks to organize it, but our family could pull off a good party in a day or two. All we had to do was to let everyone know what was planned, and decide what dish each one of us would bring to the party. Donita decided it would be at her home, since she had the in-ground pool, and we could barbeque steaks at the poolside and swim. It was late in August, so the weather would be perfect for an outdoor party. So the festivities began the weekend before he had to leave. We heartily ate baked rigatoni, seven-layer salad, and sirloin steaks from the grill. We drank plenty of wine, had cannoli for dessert, and took many pictures to remember the event. Of course I had to make seven loaves of bread for him, even though we only ate one or two. Kyle just couldn't leave without Mama's homemade bread. He packed the rest of it to take along for the ride. Kyle would be happiest if he had a few slices of salami and ham, between a hunk of bread, spread with olive oil any day. He reminded me so much of my mother in that respect. As I thought about my memories of her, I knew that she would be very proud of my kids and how well they turned out. I just wished that she could see them now, but then I had to realize that she was watching them all the time—from up above.

Kyle & Katerina at one of our family reunions

The next morning, he loaded up his little green truck, and was ready to go. I hugged him real tight and kissed him goodbye, but not before telling him how proud I was of him. I knew he would do well there. He was so happy that he finally had the chance to show the family how much money he could make without going to college. He especially wanted Donita to know that, because she was so intent on everybody having a college degree to be successful in life. Now he would have a chance at a prosperous life in the big city. At least he would be staying with his friend for a while, so I didn't have to worry so much about him. That way he could save up a little money, until he could find an apartment of his own.

During the first week there, Kyle bought a twin bed and a dresser, and set up their back den as a makeshift bedroom for himself. That way, he would be out of the way, and have a little bit of privacy. He bought a pair of good work boots and a rain slicker because the weather there was either pouring down rain or burning hot from the sun. It was always changing. He went through a week of intense training before he was able to work on his own, even though he already had railroad experience. This company was very strict about the safety rules and following the proper procedures when working on the trains. Kyle learned a lot about being a switchman/conductor there. The actual railroad yard had over one hundred miles of track. Kyle told me that this railroad company was at one of the largest ports in the United States. He loved riding the trains there, because he went places every day. He had to pick up and connect cars from all areas of the port to build the train for his load. It was very interesting to him and he never became bored with his job. He met a lot of great guys and had fun working with most of them. He would call me just about every day—either while I was at work or even in the middle of the night while I was supposed to be sleeping.

Whenever Kyle would call me, he would always say, "Hey! What's goin' on?"

It didn't matter to him if it was in the middle of the night, and I was asleep or not. When he wanted to talk to me, he would call me, even if he had to wake me up. Then I would hear a story about what had happened to him that day. He said they called him "Michigan" there. That was his nickname. He said that was their way of teasing him because he wasn't a southern boy, or a Texan. But it was all in fun. They really did like him. He told me a story about one night that he was working during a pretty bad thunderstorm. Being a switchman, he was the one who had to get off the train and connect the next car to the ones they were collecting for that shift. It was 2:00 in the morning, and it was raining pretty badly, and there was a lot of thunder and lightning. After he finally got the car connected, he had to run alongside of the slow-moving train to jump back on with the rest of the men. He was bogged down with his radio and flashlight, and soaking wet even with the slicker, so he was having trouble catching up to the ladder to get on. He was laughing so hard while he was trying to run, that his sides were hurting.

The guys kept saying, "C'mon, Michigan! You can do it! Run, Michigan, run! C'mon, Michigan, get the led out! Run, Michigan, run!"

And to hear him tell the story with his fake southern accent, was hysterical, and made me laugh too. It was so funny, until he told me that at one point, the lightning was so close that he felt it brush the back of his neck as it struck. That must have been why the guys were yelling at him to hurry and get back on the train.

This was just one incident of thunder and lightning that he told me about. There were many others, because it thundered and stormed there quite a bit, but that wasn't the only danger that he came across.

One stormy night, as he turned around to reach for the connection on another car, he came across something he never saw before, up close that is. A car that he had to retrieve was very close to a bog and swampy area. He wasn't familiar with the wild creatures that roamed around at night in Texas. He was only there about a month already, but as he turned to reach for the connections, an alligator lunged at his leg! He couldn't believe it! He wasn't warned about alligators roaming around there at night! He quickly scurried up the car's ladder, and immediately called on his radio for backup to let security know that he was in distress! Thankfully, it didn't take but a few minutes for the two men with shotguns to arrive and fire at the creature to scare it away.

Another incident was during the heat of a sunny day. He had about a quarter-mile walk to get to the two cars that he had to connect to his train that day. These two cars had not been used in quite a while, so the connections were rusted over. There also was a huge spider web between the two cars where the locking mechanisms were. As he was trying to remove the web, he was startled and had to jump back in fear. He never saw a spider the size of a pie plate before, and it almost bit him! It was so close, that he felt a furry leg brush his fingers! He still had to connect the cars, so he had to remove the spider first! When he told the guys what took him so long, they sure had a good laugh at him about that one!

There was always some excitement there that he couldn't wait to tell me about. No matter what the weather was like on a given day, there would be something exciting to report. On a sunny, hot day, while walking along the tracks, he spotted something that glistened up ahead. As he got closer to it, the more he strained in the sunlight to see what it was, it suddenly moved. By then, the toe of his boot was just inches away from a deadly copperhead snake that was stretched alongside the rail, basking in the sun! It struck at his leg, but his pant leg and boot protected him from the poisonous venom. He was so lucky. Immediately, he took off running again, back to the engine!

None of these incidents bothered him though, as much as the time he came across a dog that was killed on one of the tracks. The poor thing had to have stood there in shock, unable to move quickly as the train came upon him. I guess that is why it was so hard for Kyle to look at the poor thing. It was split right in two from the force of the engine against the rails. I could tell that he was trying to hold back his tears as he told me about it over the phone.

But when he was nearly attacked by a wild boar, he didn't feel any remorse when the security guys shot that animal! It came directly at him from under the brush one day, while he was walking the rails again. He was lucky that those security guys were right behind him, and ready to shoot this time. They knew that it was in the area, because it had tried to attack another guy earlier that week.

He also told me about the time when four or five police cars surrounded a single boxcar that he was supposed to connect. The engineer called the police to the area because Kyle told him that he saw a guy hiding in the empty car. Evidently, the cops were already looking for an escaped prisoner in the area, so when their call came through, the cops jumped at the opportunity to catch him. Kyle thought it was just like a scene in the movies, to see the capture. That made another exciting day for Kyle at work. He really loved his job there.

That summer though, I'll never forget this one phone call I got from Kyle in the middle of the night. He was so happy, but he was also crying at the time.

His call woke me up just as usual, saying, "Hey! What's goin' on?"

That was his way of saying "hello" to me all the time. Of course I told him I was sleeping, until he woke me. That didn't matter to him at all. He didn't even listen to my reply. The important thing for him to tell me was what he was doing at that very moment. Even though it was against railroad policy, Kyle told me that he was lying on his back on top of a load of PVC pipe that was in a gondola car. This car was on the train that was moving down the track at about ten miles an hour! He had no business being inside the car, but he had to do it.

He said with a quivering voice, "Mom, I see heaven! It is so beautiful! I see the stars, and beyond that, I see heaven!"

Then I heard him sobbing. All I could do was cry along with him on my end of the phone. I just listened to him talk, and pretended that I didn't know he was also crying.

As the months went by, we both were trying to adjust to the changes around us. He was trying to make a new life for himself, and I was trying to adjust to living alone, and letting him go. I think we both were quite depressed. I knew he missed home. I always asked him if he was okay.

He would reply, "Yes, but I miss the dogs and your cooking, especially the homemade bread."

I finally made him admit that he did miss Katerina and me as much as the dogs and the bread. My sisters and I sent him cards just about every week, and I always wrote a letter and enclosed it in the card. I wanted to keep our line of communication going, even without a computer and e-mail. I tried to keep myself busy at home by planting a rose garden in the back yard. I had a nice bench swing back there, and every day after work, I would go out in the back yard with the dogs and work in the yard. I checked my roses and watered all the flowers, and then I would sit on the swing and pray. Every day I cried. I asked God every day to please bring him back home. I wanted him to be happy and on his own, but I just wished that he would be close to home as well. I guess I was being selfish, but I felt so empty inside. I always dreamt of seeing him get a wife and have children that I could play with and spoil. I wanted to try to help raise them, and not make the mistakes that I made when I raised Kyle and Katerina. I wanted that chance. I don't know how I was going to live all by myself here either. Katerina always told me that she didn't want to be responsible for me in my old age, if I needed assistance. She never did like caring for older people. She just didn't seem to have the patience it required. On the other hand, Kyle loved to be around the older generation. He had a regular visiting routine, where he would stop and see many older friends here and just sit and chitchat with them and let them reminisce about the good old days. I know he missed all of his friends here too, even though he called them on a regular basis.

I think he knew that if he was going to make it down there, he had to find something there to make him happy. That is why he started looking for a place of his own. He loved his friend's children, but they were very spoiled and Kyle really didn't want to hurt his feelings by correcting them all the time. When he had to watch them on his own, he tried being strict with them, but it would just end up making them cry, and then he would feel really bad. He called me many times to tell me what they did and how he tried to correct them. He was so frustrated at times and wanted to get away from them by moving out. It especially bothered him at meal times. The two children always wanted to eat out at some fast food place, and they never seemed to agree on the same place when they went. The whole gang would drive to at least three or four different restaurants to get everybody what they wanted on a single dinner out. He couldn't believe those kids could get away with that. This went on almost every night, because his friend's wife either didn't like to cook homemade meals, or there wasn't time to cook between raising the kids, doing housework, and working a full-time job herself. So Kyle fell into the same routine with them, and ate out at What a Burger or Sonic, pretty much every night. He finally decided that if he had his own place, he could cook for himself, and save a lot of money by eating at home. After all, he was a very good cook. He made wonderful spaghetti sauce and the best fried chicken tenders you ever had. He knew how to mix up just the right seasonings to add to the flour and breading mixture, but his favorite meal to cook was a big pot of homemade chicken noodle soup with homemade noodles. He made them so tender and delicious. His cooking always impressed me. He was a natural chef. I think though, that he really missed home the most around Thanksgiving Day down there. He called me to tell me that there were only seven people there for Thanksgiving dinner and his friend's wife tried her best to cook the entire meal. He told me that she really tried hard to make a nice meal, but it was nothing like what he was used to—especially the way our family cooked. He really missed home that day.

He started to look for an apartment that would be close to the railroad yard, but apartments were so expensive in that area, so he began looking for a house to buy. In the neighboring small towns, north of Houston, there were a lot of homes that interested him, especially if they were out in the country. He wanted a little bit of land so that he could have a place to work on his antique tractors again. He loved to garden also, and that way he could make good use of a tractor. I asked him to check about getting a horse too. He loved them also, almost as much as I did. When he found a place that he thought might be right for him, he would call me at work so that I could check it out over the internet. Most of the places listed by realtors had virtual tours where one could see the rooms inside as well as outside views of the house and property.

It didn't take him very long to find a nice little brick ranch on a few acres of land with a barn and a fenced-in back yard. It was painted yellow over the brick, but he figured that he could sandblast the paint off. There also were several old pecan trees in the front yard, and about five different fruit trees in the back. It was listed at a very good price, because the little old couple that owned it was trying to sell it for several years without any luck, until they lowered the asking price. Now all Kyle had to do was to get approved for the loan. I wasn't sure that financially, he would qualify, but he did make pretty good money there.

It was right before Christmas that his loan was accepted and he made plans to move. He was so funny. Every day he called me and told me about the ducks and the geese he was going to get for the back yard. The only problem that he told me about would be the creatures that crawled in the grass in Texas. It was nothing like what we have here in our city yards. He told me that if I walked in the yard there, I might see a snake or a scorpion, since it was out in the country. I didn't like hearing that, but he also knew where to find a couple of nice horses for the barn, and that really enticed me to move there with him. He knew I would want to move there if he bought horses, so he planned to get them. Naturally, I worried that he would overspend though, just to get everything he wanted right away. He was very compulsive in that respect. But the more and more he told me about the place, the more I wanted to go down there and help him paint and decorate. I loved to do that sort of thing. I felt that if I was there to help, that I could also cook and clean and do the laundry for him again. I really wanted to move down there with him, but I didn't want him to feel like he was a mama's boy, and needed me to run to his side. I waited to see if he would ask me to come, and he did, just as I thought. I guess he knew that he still would need to take care of me as I got older. So moving down there with him, so that I could help, would be good for both of us. I would have easily quit my job in a minute to move to Texas, just to be near him.

Katerina always said that she would like to live down there also. That would be a good excuse for all of us to be together again. I would want to be there when he would get married and start a family, just as I would also want to be there for Katerina. We have always been a very close-knit family and never had any trouble communicating with each other. I guess that is a characteristic of our Italian heritage. But for now, I still was unsure of my security in my old age, financially and emotionally. I have always worried about living alone, especially if I were to have health issues later on in life. I know that Kyle worried about me also in that respect, but somehow, he felt that this move would be the best thing to do right then. He was so excited about becoming a homeowner. The little old couple that lived there were very nice to Kyle. They had dinner together and the old man told Kyle everything about the house and how to care for things in the proper way. Kyle also helped them find an apartment in a senior housing development so they wouldn't have the burden of cutting grass anymore. Kyle even helped them move all their belongings to their new place, right before Christmas. Kyle had a very quiet Christmas though with his friend's family. He made sure to buy some nice toys for the kids and something special for the family because of all the help they gave him. But even though his Christmas present to himself was a house, he was very sad and missed home. He called me that evening and I could tell that he had been crying. He said he missed the snow. But I knew it wasn't just the snow. It was his dog, and his family that he missed the most, and of course, the food.

The day that was scheduled for the closing was going to be the Thursday right after Christmas. He had a couple of days off in between Christmas and the New Year, so it would work out fine. But when he went into work on one of his days off to pick up his schedule for the next week, he found out that he might be laid off after Christmas. He was devastated. He knew that there was no way that he could sign the papers for the house now. It would be too risky if he were to be laid off—even if it was temporary.

Again he called me, but with better news. He wasn't crying this time. He told me that he had a talk with his supervisor at work and asked for a forty-five-day leave of absence. Giada was very ill and was having a very serious operation, so he felt he needed to be there because he was very close to my sister. She has always been like a second mother to him. It was a good excuse, because it really was true, but he told them she was his grandmother, instead of his aunt. He thought that would make it a better excuse to leave. Giada had to have an operation to repair her esophagus because of the damage caused to it from achalasia. It is a very rare disease where a part of the esophagus closes off to the point that a person can't eat and even has trouble swallowing water. She lost about one hundred pounds since the disease started, and so it was very necessary to operate because she was wasting away to nothing. He didn't want to really let his boss know quite yet, but he already made another decision. He was not going to buy that house or any house down there. He was coming home, but not just for a visit. He was coming home for good! God answered my prayers. He was moving back home with me!

Chapter Seven

Keepsakes

It was easy for him to say goodbye to Texas. It was the first day of the New Year. It was going to be the first day of another fresh start for him. He knew that he could find something—anything, so that he could stay home. Home, just the thought of it made him happy. He longed for home. He missed the cold. He loved the crisp, fresh air of winter. He loved to see the snow falling, and didn't mind when a snowflake clung to his eyelashes, or his ears turned red and burned from the cold air. He couldn't wait to get his tractor out of the garage and push the snow out of the driveway at our home and many of the neighbors' homes as well. He really enjoyed doing it and didn't want any payment for clearing all the driveways on our street.

Packing was easy for him. He left the bed and dresser there. All he took were his clothes and personal possessions. He simply threw them all into any cardboard box he could find, and taped them up with duct tape, and threw them into the back of his truck. He put a plastic tarp over the truck bed, and tied it down with a nylon rope so he wouldn't lose anything on the long drive home. The only thing he kept on the front seat with him was his huge collection of classical and liturgical CD's that he could sing along with as he drove.

I got busy in the kitchen and made his favorite foods to greet him when he got back. I baked his seven loaves of Italian bread, a pan of lasagna with lots of Italian sausage and pepperoni in it, and an apple pie with a thick crust. I knew he would be hungry when he arrived. I called him every couple of hours, just to make sure he was still awake, and to find out how far along he was on the road home. He would have to stop somewhere halfway to sleep, because he couldn't make the twenty-one-hour drive all the way home in one day. So he stopped to sleep for about six hours very late that night at a rest stop, and continued home early the next morning. He hoped to arrive home by about one or two the following morning, which would be on the third of January. I was so excited that I slept in the living room on the Lazy Boy chair in front of the television. I wanted to be right by the door when he arrived. Just having him back home would be a late Christmas present for me, but the best present I could have asked for.

I awoke to the sound of the dogs barking at around one-thirty in the morning. They always barked when they heard a vehicle pull into our driveway. But when I went to the window to look for Kyle's little green truck, I was surprised to see a newer-looking, white truck instead. I thought at first that maybe someone else had pulled in the drive, but then I saw him get out. It was Kyle all right. But where was his little green truck? He was grinning from ear to ear as he came up the front steps to the door. When he came in I gave him a big hug and kissed his cheek as I asked him whose truck he was driving. Then he told me that he traded in his little green truck for a brand-new, bigger white truck. I was shocked! He actually made this purchase all on his own and never told anyone about it, or asked anyone in the family for their opinion before he did it! I guess he probably knew that all of us would simply tell him that he was already deep enough in debt. I just shook my head and wondered how he was going to pay for it, especially since he gave up his job to come home now. It was just going to be one more thing that I would worry about for him. He was much too easy going, and never seemed to worry enough about finances until they became overwhelming. That was Kyle's free spirit. He loved life, and lived his life to the fullest, and made each day a vibrant one. That was his motto.

Before he could walk any further into the house, his dog Sonoma and my dog Simon tackled him to the ground with their tails wagging furiously. He was laughing and crying at the same time, while they both were licking his face and barking with excitement. I don't know who was happier at the greeting—the dogs seeing Kyle, or Kyle seeing the dogs! It took a few minutes for all three of them to settle down so he could go back outside and gather up the boxes of clothing in the back of the truck. He dropped them all in the middle of the living room floor with a sigh of relief. He finally made it back home. Then he smelled the food and went straight into the kitchen. He was thrilled with the bread and lasagna that I made for him and dove right in. With each mouthful he swallowed, he would tell me about something more that happened to him in Texas. He was talking so fast while he was devouring his food that he quickly became very tired. He almost fell asleep right in his chair in the kitchen, so I coaxed him up to his room. He would have to go through his belongings the next day. I didn't care if he left me a mess. I was glad that he was safely home. As I put all the food away, I thanked God for answering my prayers.

The next afternoon, when I came home from work, he had already gone out somewhere. I assumed that he dropped in on some of his old friends, and was also out looking for work. When he came back home later that night, he told me that one of his old buddies heard about an opening at a railroad nearby, and was also going to apply for the position. That didn't bother Kyle at all. He would just try to do his best and hope and pray that he would be hired. This company was in a transition that would develop a new type of system transport with more commodities to other locations. This would require the laying of new track and more employees to carry out the process, so it was probable that more than one person would be hired. Kyle was so excited about the news and went the very next day to talk to someone to set up an interview. He was excited that this company was downriver and only about thirty-five minutes from home.

The next morning, it was sheer luck that the human resources director happened to be available when Kyle went into the office to apply. He ended up talking to the guy for quite a long while. The man was very impressed with Kyle's knowledge of the railroad—especially at such a young age. Kyle told me that this guy kept saying that he felt like he was talking to an old man ready to retire, instead of a young man of twenty-four. He couldn't figure out how Kyle knew so much about railroad work, and had a good answer for every question that he threw at him. He especially liked the fact that Kyle had been very well trained in the safety that is involved in being a switchman/conductor. That was very important to both of them. He was just beaming with excitement when he told me that he was going back there the next day to take a written exam, and get a physical with the company doctor. He would also have to demonstrate some actual manual and safety procedures properly, before he would be considered for the position. But Kyle was very sure of himself, and knew that he would do just fine. It seemed that everything was working in his favor this time.

He stayed close by the phone for the next couple of days. He was anxious to hear from them about the position again soon. The next afternoon, the human resources director finally called and informed Kyle that he would start work there at the beginning of the following week! He was told that he would be working while training with one of the older, more experienced switchman for about six weeks, before he would be allowed to work on his own. That was the proper procedure at any railroad. Kyle was thrilled and immediately took off to tell his friends that he made it. I was happy for him too. He would be making a lot of money, and finally be able to get on top of his bills.

During the next few weeks, the work/training days were easy for Kyle. He was good at listening to orders and following proper procedure. He got along fine with the older conductor that he worked with, and the other employees that worked with him knew that Kyle was very serious and professional about his job, even though he was the youngster in the yard. Safety was the most important thing when working on the railroad. He had to be alert at all times and always follow proper procedures to be safe.

When he finally finished his training and was allowed to work on his own, he was put up on the call board, which meant that he could be called in to work at any time to replace someone that called in sick or would be taking a vacation day. He kept his cell phone charged and with him all the time. I didn't think that this type of arrangement would give him much work, but I was wrong. He seemed to be scheduled to work almost every day. He told me that was the way he worked in Texas also, so it was nothing new to him. It was a good job with decent pay, and he seemed content for a while, but after a couple of months, I knew he wasn't really all that happy. I asked him how he was doing, one day when I came home and found him upstairs on the computer. I could tell he was very upset about something. He told me that he was written up for a safety violation! Some of the guys told him that he was not using the proper foot on ascending and descending the railcar ladder. Kyle was very upset. He was sure he was doing it right. He insisted that he was doing it the way he was taught in Texas and that was at a higher-class railroad than here. The Texas railroad job was also part of the same union that was at this railroad yard. He got on the web and actually found a video clip that showed the proper mounting and dismounting procedure of the ladder. He showed me the clip in slow motion and pointed out which foot the guy was using first. Kyle was doing it right according to the video, so he copied it on a disk and brought it to work. The foreman actually scheduled a meeting with all the employees to discuss the ladder procedure because Kyle was so adamant about it. He showed them the video clip and after discussing it with everyone for a while, Kyle was told that he could use whichever foot he was most comfortable using to mount and dismount the ladder. Kyle had made his case and the safety grievance was thrown out!

This really wasn't the reason though that Kyle was unhappy. He hesitated a little before he told me that the job was monotonous to him. This rail yard amounted to only about five miles of track, but he was actually used to traveling somewhere on the rail cars when he collected them for a train, since the Texas yard had over one hundred miles of track. This was quite a big difference in size and in daily work experiences. Then he told me that he started looking into another railroad here that worked as a type of commuter train that traveled through several small towns and back again, on a daily basis. At least that way he could be going somewhere and seeing different things every day. It would make it more interesting to handle different types of rail cars with different types of commodities in them. At least for now he had a job, and he wasn't going to quit it, unless he was sure to be hired somewhere else.

When Kyle knew he wouldn't be working the next day, he would meet his old buddy, Sam, after Sam got off work. That usually would be around 11:30 at night. They started meeting for coffee at the neighborhood Danny's restaurant to catch up on what was going on in each other's lives. News traveled fast that Kyle was back in town, and so a lot of other guys and gals stopped in there to see him and chat. Pretty soon, they developed a small group that met there late at night at least once a week. Wilma, the restaurant manager, had no problem with them meeting there and having coffee and talking for hours. She felt that since it was during the late shift when it was pretty slow, they could sit there and talk all they wanted to. At least that way they were not going to get into any trouble doing something else. Sometimes they talked until 2:00 a.m., but she enjoyed seeing them and listening to them converse, because they were all such a nice group of kids. Most of the time, the conversations would drift toward a religious theme, especially if Kyle had something to say. Pretty soon, he and Sam were leading an actual Bible study with the group, and they were all enjoying it! That was typical of Kyle and Sam. It seemed that both of them would always have something to say that would lead to a heavy discussion pertaining to religion. Kyle could evangelize all he wanted, and his other friends loved to listen to him and share their thoughts on religion as well. They really were an impressive group of young adults.

Kyle devoted his time between work and family and friends. If he wasn't working, he was hanging out with the guys at the restaurant, or visiting someone in our family. He would stay over at Ned's house some nights, if they were playing cards or watching movies late. Ned bought a house in the country after he got married and Kyle loved to be out there with him too. Of course, he kept trying to convince Ned that he should get a tractor and do a little farming. Most of the time, I never really knew where Kyle was anymore. But then a family member or old friend would call me to tell me about their visit from Kyle. Uncle Mac always called me after Kyle stopped in to visit with him. He saw Kyle just about every week. Kyle loved to visit with Uncle Mac because he was a retired railroad man and the two of them had a lot of stories to tell each other about the railroad. Kyle always made a good impression on

Uncle Mac, and that made me feel pretty good. Sometimes they would reminisce for hours about old times and railroad life. Everywhere he went someone eventually would let me know that they saw Kyle and had a nice visit with him. They always had such nice things to say about Kyle, and that made me very proud of my son.

I remember the nice time we had, one Saturday in February, when I didn't have to work and Kyle also was home. He asked me if I would like to go for a ride with him in his new truck. I was delighted, and jumped at the chance, because he said he would take me to an Italian specialty store in a town nearby. It was a little drive, but it would give us a chance to talk. Even though it snowed recently, and a soft, white blanket covered the ground, the warm sun made it feel like a summer day. It seemed like we talked about everything that day. I mentioned his finances, and tried to coax him into managing them better. We talked about cooking, and special recipes that he also enjoyed. I tried to find out if he had an interest in any particular girl since he had returned home, but he really couldn't say. We also played our favorite music game as he drove. He would play a certain CD and I would have to guess who the composer was or what piece it was, or what type of music it was. He loved to try to fool me—especially if it was either a Mozart or Salieri CD. He had a special interest in Salieri because they were both born on the same day in August. Kyle collected just as many CD's by that composer as I did by Mozart. He always had me guessing. Even though I was a music teacher before he was born, he could stil stump me.

When we finally got to the little Italian store, it had already closed so we drove back home, but not without stopping for his favorite fast food burger first. When we finally were near our street though, he decided not to go directly home, but to drive around our old neighborhood. I thought it was strange, but he wanted to reminisce about his years growing up there. He brought up the time when he stopped on his bike to pick up broken glass on the sidewalk, so the other kids wouldn't step on it, or ride their bikes over it. I remember that a neighbor lady came over that day to tell me how impressed she was with Kyle, when she saw him do that. Chuckling, he reminded me of the day that he and Ned shot those paint balls all over the back fence and the garage door! He said that he was really sorry about doing that. He also reminded me of the time he tried to remove some of the wood molding on the staircase in the basement because he was looking for hidden treasure! He just shook his head and laughed at himself while he apologized for that incident too. He brought up the many times that he coaxed Katerina into riding her bike down to the corner store to get candy for all the kids. She was always an easy mark when it came to sweets. He could get her to do anything for chocolate! He also apologized for spinning her around on the front porch until she passed out and hit her forehead on the iron railing. She did get a pretty big scar from that little game, and he really regretted doing that to her. He went on and on about all those little things, and then he said something that I would never, ever forget. He told me that through it all—good times and bad—I was always there for him and for Katerina. He said that he was very proud to have me for his mother. He said I did the best job of raising him and Katerina that any mother could ever have done. I didn't know what to say or think. I just sat there with tears rolling down my cheeks, and when I looked over at him, I could see tears welling up in his eyes also. I really couldn't understand why he wanted to tell me all of that, but it ended up being the best day I ever spent with Kyle.

On St. Patrick's Day in March, Kyle, Katerina, and I had to have our little traditional celebration at home, before the two of them went out to the pub to drink with their friends. I had to make my special corned beef sandwiches and Kyle would go to the store and buy the Guinness for us to drink. We would all sit down and watch the movie *Darby O'Gill and the Little People* together. Then Kyle would entertain us with his version of Irish brogue. He could tell a little joke or sing a little song, while sounding like he just got off the boat from Dublin! He was very entertaining, and we could listen to him for hours, but he would tease us with just a little bit of Irish charm.

Later on that month, I came home from work early one day, and was surprised at the sight I saw. As soon as I was in the door, I smelled the delicious aroma of chicken soup simmering on the stove, and found Kyle running the vacuum cleaner on the kitchen counter! Kyle loved to cook and he made wonderful chicken noodle soup. However, he made such a mess doing it. Sometimes I didn't know if it was worth having him cook because of the mess that he made! He always made the noodles from scratch right on the kitchen counter. He would pour out a measure of flour and make a well and work the eggs right into it. However, I didn't know until that day, that he was using the vacuum cleaner to clean up his mess! But I guess I had to overlook the mess because nobody could make a pot of chicken soup like Kyle. The noodles were always so tender and the broth was very flavorful with carrots, celery, parsley, and paprika in it. He used nothing but the best ingredients and would go right to the butcher and get a whole chicken just for the stock. Nobody in our family could make it any better.

By early March, Kyle started getting phone calls from creditors and I seemed to be the only one who was there when they called. Of course, they wouldn't tell me what the calls were about, as much as I wanted to know. They could only discuss finances with him. So when I got the chance to ask him about it, I did. Of course, he would only smile and tell me that there was nothing wrong financially, and that I shouldn't worry so much. But the calls kept coming, and even Giada asked me how he was doing with his bills because she worried about him too. He wouldn't talk to her over the phone either. He just kept saying he would talk to her when she came back from Florida, and that hurt her feelings. I think she had a premonition that something was wrong. So I kept asking him, and Giada kept asking me. Finally, I told her to stop, because he told me that everything was fine. But wouldn't you know it, that very same day, one of the creditors finally hinted to me that they were coming to repossess his new white truck! I was furious with him, and he knew it when I confronted him with that news! So I immediately called Giada back and let her know that she was right and that he was in big trouble. So again, Giada and Leonardo wired the money to the finance company for the two payments that he was behind on. He had only made the first initial payment on the truck, and nothing more! If my sister hadn't kept bugging me to find out, Kyle would have lost the truck, and then he wouldn't have had a way to get to his job. Sometimes he just didn't use his head. He would have had the money to pay for it, if he wouldn't have been so frivolous. Money simply slipped through his fingers, and he didn't seem to have a care in the world. I guess he was never going to learn, but luckily my sister cared enough to keep after him.

When my sister and brother-in-law came back home from Florida the first week in April, Kyle went over to see them and thank them in person for all their help. He also wrote them a little note that he mailed to them in Florida the week before.

Unc & GG,

Thanks for the help. I was really hangin' on by a thin thread. Thank God I finally got hired. You both know that I am not a big phone talker. Come home and we can talk in person.

Love Ya'll,

Kyle

With his charming personality and smiling face to greet them, they soon forgave him for not talking to them over the phone since Christmas. He had that Irish sparkle in his eyes and that cute little grin that would melt your heart and soothe away any grievance that you would have with him. He definitely was a real charmer.

He stopped in to see Giada and Leonardo, or Unc and GG, as he called them, on his way home from work, just about every day then to make up for the lost time. He especially wanted to talk with Unc one day, but he was over at Patrice's house, painting her living room. Giada asked Kyle if he wanted to go over there and help his uncle out.

But all he could say was, "Nah, GG. I don't do painting," as he leaned back in Unc's favorite leather Lazy Boy chair.

She thought it quite funny to hear him say that. She remembered the time that Kyle purchased all that equipment, right down to the white overalls, so that he could be a professional painter. You would think that he would have jumped at the chance to show off his expertise in that area! Of course, if he were asked to help Leonardo with the tractor, or the front-end loader, he would be on his feet in no time, ready to work.

Then there was the day that Giada asked him to go out and help Unc and little Drew plant the garden.

All he could say was, "Nah, GG. I don't do gardens."

She commented to Leonardo that she felt that Kyle had become somewhat lazy, but Leonardo was insistent that he was not lazy at all. He considered Kyle to be very helpful as far as he was concerned. When Unc asked Kyle to help him dig a ditch in the back forty, he jumped at the chance to help. No matter how hot it was or how difficult the task was, if Unc asked Kyle to help him, Kyle was there on the spot, and worked without a single complaint. We all knew that Kyle would do anything for Unc, if he asked him to. Kyle actually thought of Unc as the father figure that seemed to be missing in his life. Giada thought that since she was so close to Kyle, and she felt so special to him, that maybe he thought of her as his mother too. So she asked him one day, as he was hugging her goodbye, if that was the way he felt.

He adamantly replied, "Nah, GG. I have a mother. I couldn't ask for a better mother than the one I have. But you are my grandma, and you'll always be my grandma."

She just smiled at him and didn't say anything more.

She had become the grandma in his life, since my mother died when Kyle was only five. Of course, Unc and GG loved him as the son that they never had, and would give Kyle a financial lecture every chance they could, but I think that it just went in one ear and out the other. He just couldn't save a penny.

At the beginning of May, my sister Giada finally had the operation on her esophagus for the achalasia. Her esophagus was almost completely closed off by the time she had to wait for her scheduled operation. It took such a long time to find a surgeon who was familiar with her disease, and confident enough to do the repairs. I remember seeing her choke even when she tried to drink a cup of hot tea. It was awful and we were so worried about her. We were glad that she finally was able to get a specialist to do the operation. He removed a section of her esophagus and reattached it to her stomach and then stretched out the rest of the esophagus so that she could eat again. We were so relieved when it was all over and she began to feel better again. We knew that she felt better when she started to cook her special meatballs and sauce again. She wanted to make sure that we had all the best foods prepared for little Drew's First Communion party.

She cleaned and pressed his suit and polished his shoes to help Marie get him ready. This suit was handed down to him from his father and his uncle who also wore it for their First Communion day. It actually was over fifty years old, but was kept in very good condition. It had white linen pants and a white linen jacket. Drew was the only boy wearing all white, but he was proud to wear it because it was his father's suit before him. All of us were taught that tradition played a very important part in our family, and Drew knew that he was going to be extra special that day because of his suit. He looked just like an angel with his tiny frame and platinum blonde hair.

All the family made sure to be there at the church and for his party afterwards, but Kyle came very early. He went over to see Giada that morning to visit with her while she was working on the suit and cooking the meatballs. He had a lot of time before the celebration, so after talking to Giada for a while, he went over to visit Uncle Mat, since he lived close by. After visiting with Uncle Mat for a while, it was still early, so Kyle went back over to help Giada bring the food over to Marie's house to get the party set up. He loved parties, but especially family gatherings and celebrations. To him, a First Communion party was the most important type of celebration to have. Naturally, with our Italian family there was plenty of homemade wine to go with the many flavorful Italian dishes that Giada and Marie prepared. Our family never scrimped when it came to food and wine. Rochelle's husband Ben was the family expert on winemaking. He enjoyed making it and everyone loved the different types of wine that he brought to our parties.

Kyle was the first one to open a bottle and try out one of the blends that Ben had brought. He didn't have much self-control when there was homemade wine around. He also knew that the family would let him drink as much as he wanted. Ben and Rochelle were very generous, and it made Ben feel so good when people complimented him on the wine that he made. Everyone loved to see Kyle get a little tipsy too. He was a great entertainer when he had a few drinks under his belt, and this time was no exception.

Kyle celebrating at a family party

Before all the food was set out, Kyle already had enough to drink, so we all coaxed him into eating something to sober up a little. He was so funny though, especially when someone got him to sing a little tune. He would put on an Irish brogue that would sound quite convincing, but before we could get him to take a little nap, he started to have a serious talk with Drew. I think it started with religion and how important his First Communion day should be and what it meant to be able to receive the Lord. Then they talked about all the other boys and girls in the family and when they made their First Communion. Drew thought that Rochelle's son Nate was the first to make his because he was Giada's oldest grandchild, but Kyle quickly corrected him. He always felt that Giada was his grandmother too because of the way she loved him so much and how close they were to each other. He quickly and adamantly corrected him.

With a stern, deep voice, he said, "I was GG's first grandchild, Drew! Remember what I tell you! I was before Nate, and I was before Donny, I was before Scotty and Zeb, and I was before you! I was GG's first! Remember this. I was GG's first!"

Poor Drew just looked at him sheepishly and said, "Okay Kyle," and walked away.

Then Kyle went into Drew's bedroom and crawled onto his little twin bed and took a good nap.

A couple of days later, Kyle and I were standing in the kitchen as he got a glass of milk from the fridge. We both had just arrived home from work, but he got there about fifteen minutes before me. I was looking over the mail and he was leaning back on the counter over the sink. As he was drinking the glass of milk, I could tell that he wanted to talk to me about something.

Worriedly, he looked at me and said, "Mom, please don't be sad when I die on the railroad."

I looked at him in terror and said, "Kyle! What are you saying? Don't talk like that! Why are you talking about death? You are following all the safety rules, aren't you?"

He just nodded yes and didn't answer me, but I was so shocked at what he said. I quickly went over to him and hugged him around the waist.

Then I said, "Please, Kyle, you have to be very careful there!"

He just said quietly, "I am."

Then the subject was dropped. I didn't want to even think about it at all. The thought of him being in such a dangerous place made me very nervous, so I blocked it out of my mind. I couldn't believe that he could say such a thing to me. I just wanted to forget it completely.

Knowing how much our family loves to eat, my sister always had something cooking in her kitchen. When you walked in the door from the garage, the first breath that you inhaled would fill your nasal passages with the savory aroma of some delectable dish. She especially loved to make all kinds of soups or pasta sauces, and kept them simmering on the stove for hours. Kyle knew this about my sister, and I think that is why he would stop in at her house, instead of coming right home from work sometimes. Except for the homemade bread that I made for him, Giada loved the fact that Kyle would want to eat her cooking over mine. She could tell how hungry he was by the way he called out to her as he walked into the kitchen. The higher the pitch, or the louder he sang out her name, would alert her to how much he needed nourishment. That's the way it was that afternoon.

As he came in her door, he excitedly yelled out, "Schgee Schgeeeee! Schgee Schgeeeee!"

But she didn't return his greeting right away. That was her cue to put a bowl of something in front of him first, and then greet him with a kiss and a hug.

That was how it was that day, when she made the cauliflower soup. When he came in, Giada noticed that his overalls were filthy and his face was still black from the soot at work. While she was getting his bowl, she sent him directly into the bathroom to wash his face, but when he came out she could still see the black soot around his eyes. It looked as though he had mascara on, but she didn't tell him that because she didn't want to hurt his feelings. So while he was waiting for the soup to be warmed up a little, he devoured a piece of angel food cake and some red diet Jello with fruit cocktail and whipped cream. It was supposed to be for his dessert, but he was famished and ate it right down. As soon as she set the soup in front of him, he dove right in.

But after a couple of spoonfuls, he stopped and exclaimed to her, "Schgee Schgeee! Panera doesn't have anything over on you! This soup is the best I have ever tasted! Wow!"

Giada just smiled and told him that she put a bit of Cajun spice in it along with some ham, cheese, and a few potatoes. She loved to make up her own recipes when she cooked, and this one turned out to be exceptional.

When he finished two bowls full, he asked her for another one to take home, but Giada told him she had to save some for Unc for his supper. So for consolation, she asked him what he wanted to have the next day. He told her that he wanted her to make him some vegetable beef stew with lots of big chunks of beef in it. He was glad to hear that she agreed to do it, so he got up from the table and went into the family room to relax on Unc's favorite Lazy Boy chair. She didn't say anything to him, but she noticed that he still had on his dirty work boots, besides those filthy overalls. But when he went to sit down, he realized how dirty his boots were, so he went back to the door and took them off.

After relaxing in the chair for a while, he started reading the daily newspaper. He looked at the obituaries and noticed that his best friend, Sam's, grandfather died. He said something to Giada about him, and she told him that he should go to the funeral to give some support to his friend.

But he looked at her and calmly said, "Nah, GG. I don't do funerals."

Then she questioned him saying, "Are you going to go to my funeral when I die?"

But he just looked at her with an empty expression in his eyes, and then went back to reading the paper.

Before leaving for home, he hugged her and kissed her twice. He asked her if she was going to be okay now that she had her surgery, and she told him that she was fine and not to worry. Then she hugged him again and said goodbye.

When he arrived home, I was getting ready to cook dinner, but he told me that he had already eaten at G's house. Then he proceeded to tell me how great the soup was that she fed him. He went on and on, bragging about her food, but all I could say was that my sister was spoiling him, especially when he was ordering meals that he wanted her to cook the next day! That was part of Kyle's charm though. Kyle knew that with a few compliments and his charming smile, he could get people to do exactly what he wanted. He was spoiled, but that was okay. We all loved him so much that it didn't really matter what he asked.

Since I didn't have to cook any dinner, I grabbed a sandwich and a glass of milk and went out into the back yard to work up the soil by the fence. I wanted to plant some rose bushes back there so I needed to get the soil prepared. Kyle was working on his tractor in the garage. Soon, I heard the engine running, and then he began to drive the tractor out onto the driveway. I hoped that he would stay on the pavement because the grass was still tender and some patches were still just sprouting back. But before I could go back to my flowerbeds, he drove onto the lawn! There he was, sitting tall in the seat, grinning from ear to ear, driving around in circles, as he made tire ruts on the tender grass! It reminded me of the character on the old *Green Acres* television show. He was so happy, and I hated to burst his bubble. I just didn't want him to kill the new grass, so I yelled at him to get off the lawn. But he just grinned at me and said that he could drive it around the lawn all he wanted. I knew that I couldn't stop him so I just dropped it.

Then I saw where he fixed the spot where my flower box sat between the gate and the neighbor's fence. That place was just built up with bricks and they were always leaning or falling over. But he had taken some cement blocks and leveled it off and stacked them so they wouldn't fall. He placed the flower box on top of it all and it looked great. I was so surprised and happy that he fixed it for me, so I ran over to him and thanked him. I told him how nice it was and what a great job he did on it. He just smiled down at me and drove the tractor around the lawn again. Then I went to the front yard and began working on the flowerbed under the weeping cherry tree. I was down on my knees, working up the soil, when I saw him come up to talk to me again.

He knelt down close to me and said in a soft, concerned tone, "Mom, please don't be sad when I die on the railroad."

Again I yelled, "Stop it, Kyle! Stop it! Don't talk like that!"

He said softly, "But I just don't want you to be sad!"

I stood up and looked at him sternly and said, "Please stop thinking about dying because it makes me nervous and scared!"

So he didn't say anything more to me. He just turned around, and with a worried look on his face, walked back to the garage, and put his tractor away.

That evening, I went to bed around eight because I knew I had to get up at five the next morning for work. Kyle went out about the same time to one of his friends' houses to play some cards. I woke up around eleven because I heard him come back home. I had to go to the bathroom anyway. I always woke up easily if someone opened the front door, because the dogs would bark. The next morning, I got up and got the coffee going and fixed Kyle some oatmeal at the usual time. He liked it fixed with brown sugar, a little cream, and a pat of real butter on top. He seemed very quiet when he came down for breakfast that morning. We sat and ate breakfast together, but didn't talk, so I went up to take my shower. He had already taken his shower and dressed before he came down. But while I was still in the shower, I heard the front door open and close again. I figured that he left for work, but I felt bad that we didn't even talk much that morning; and he never even said goodbye before he left.

Chapter Eight

Realities

It was Friday and I overheard that the boss was letting us go at 3:00 p.m. I was so glad. It was such a beautiful spring day and I couldn't wait to go shopping. All I had to do was pass out the payroll checks at noon to the employees and then I would be out the door by 3:00. But I didn't know that there was a couple out in the greenhouse shopping, until they stopped in the office to settle their bill. It was almost 3:00 p.m., so I hoped that I could take care of them quickly so that I could be off. I hated it when people just showed up and decided to walk around the greenhouse and then buy flowers. The greenhouse was supposed to be strictly wholesale, but some people felt that they could do whatever they wanted, especially if they were rich and had the money to spend. That was the case with this funeral director and his wife who showed up that day. They were not regular customers, but since they would be paying with a credit card, we couldn't say anything. I just hated people like that, and I especially hated funeral directors because I didn't like thinking about death. Seeing them there in my office reminded me of every funeral that I had ever been to and everyone that I had lost. It just felt so creepy to me to be around them, so I took care of them politely and quickly, and then I was out the door a little after 3:00 p.m.

My first stop was at the grocery store and then I would stop in at the garden center and pick out some rose bushes. I couldn't wait to start planting them in the back yard along the fence line. I picked out a couple of fragrant pink tea roses, and a beautiful deep red one to go in front of the purple clematis that was growing so well there by the gate. By 3:45, I had everything in the car and was ready to head home. I tried to call Kyle on my cell phone before I left the parking lot so he would be ready to bring everything in the house for me. I knew he would be getting off work at 3:30, so he would be home around 4:00 p.m. to help me, but he didn't answer his cell phone or the home phone. So I left a message on both phones, hoping that he would retrieve them soon, and be ready to help me bring everything in.

As I pulled in the driveway after my ten-minute drive home, it was a depressing sight to see it empty, so I knew I would have to bring everything in myself. After I put all the groceries away, I tried to call Kyle again on his cell phone, but I had to leave another message. I couldn't figure out why he wasn't answering his phone. I never had to leave messages before. He always answered his phone right away, and especially on Fridays. He was usually home right away after doing his banking and he knew that I would be bringing home food. He loved to go through the bags to see what I bought, because I always brought home something special, just for him. He loved food, and it made me feel good to cook for him because he always complimented me on what I prepared. A little while later, I went upstairs to get on the computer and check my e-mail. I also thought I might as well kill some time and check out my favorite web sites while I was up there. I didn't want to make any dinner yet, because I wasn't sure when he would be home, or if he already had dinner with a friend. Sometimes he neglected to call me and let me know if his plans had been changed.

The beautiful sunny day that started out so great, suddenly became gloomy, gray, and rainy. It was about 6:00 p.m. when I heard a knock at the door. I wondered who could be coming over at this hour. When I opened the door, there stood my sister Giada and my nieces, Marie and Patrice. What a nice surprise! But by the look on their faces, I knew that something was wrong.

Quickly, I said, "What's wrong? Is it Kyle! What happened! He's dead isn't he?"

Giada spoke first, and in a very sorrowful tone, she said, "There's been an accident and we think Kyle is dead."

I screamed, "Goddam railroad! Goddam son-of-a-bitchin' railroad! No! No! Not my Kyle!"

We grabbed each other and began to weep and wail. She said she heard from her neighbor that there was an accident at the railroad yard where Kyle worked. Her neighbor's nephew had called to let him know what he heard from a coworker. He told Giada that the coworker said there was a derailment at the factory and a man named Kyle was either hurt or possibly killed.

I screamed again and said, "No! It can't be!"

My sister and nieces were also sobbing and crying, and all four of us were trying to hold each other for comfort. I was numb and in shock. I just couldn't believe what I was hearing!

I shook my head and screamed again, "My Kyle! My only son! My baby! How could this be? He told me he was safe! He was so adamant about following safety procedures there! This has to be a mistake!"

Marie went to the phone and started calling information to get some phone numbers for the railroad yard to see if she could get some answers. Patrice used her cell phone and called the hospitals in the area to see if he possibly had been admitted. We all hoped that maybe he was just hurt and not really killed. I heard Marie talk to somebody at the bridge or at the rail yard, and they wouldn't tell her anything. She always was a very calm person, but this time she actually started yelling at the man on the other end of the phone because he wouldn't tell her anything.

She said in a very loud and angry voice, "If it was your son, wouldn't you want to know what happened to him?"

Still though, he wouldn't tell her anything.

Patrice wasn't getting anywhere with the hospitals either. So I went upstairs to the computer and looked on the web site to see if there was another phone number for the rail yard that I could call. My heart was racing and my hands were shaking. I could feel the throbbing pulse in my neck, and I felt like I could hardly breathe. My stomach was in knots and I wanted to throw up. I thought that since nobody had called me, it must be a mistake! I felt a great heaviness in my chest like my heart was actually in pain. Surely someone there would let me know what happened! I couldn't find anything on the computer, so I went down the stairs to the kitchen and started screaming at the top of my lungs again. I took a frying pan and started beating it against the kitchen counter as I screamed and yelled every profanity that I could think of. I didn't care if I broke the pan or chipped the counter. I was boiling over with anger.

I yelled and screamed in anger at the top of my lungs, "How could you? God! How could you do this to me?"

My mind was racing, and then I thought to myself. God had already taken my father when he was only thirty-nine and I was just an eighteen-month-old baby! I never really had a father and my mother was already dead, and now He has to take my only son too! What have I done to deserve all of this! And to top it all off, it was actually Friday the thirteenth, and the week of Mother's Day!

Then I said out loud, "Thanks a lot, God! What a present!"

The next three hours were a blur. By the time I was contacted by the railroad, it was 9:00 p.m. I was told that Kyle died at 3:15 p.m. and I was left wondering where my son was from 4:00 p.m. until 6:00 p.m., and then we were all frantic for well over three hours after that! When the railroad supervisor finally came to my door at 9:00 p.m., the reality of Kyle's death finally sank in. Kyle's supervisor didn't really have to say anything to confirm it, but he told me how sorry he was and that he didn't want to tell me anything over the phone. His wife accompanied him, and he could barely walk up the steps.

He wanted to talk to me in person. He told me that he would never forget Kyle and how impressed he was with him as an employee at the railroad, and what a wonderful young man he was. He remembered his first meeting with Kyle and how much knowledge Kyle had about railroad work. He felt so bad that the accident had occurred, but especially that it had to be Kyle that was killed. Kyle had so much potential and so much zest for life. He said that all the workers and the management there were devastated at Kyle's death. Then we all stood in the middle of the living room, held hands in a circle, and the supervisor's wife lead a prayer for Kyle.

After that I had a few questions to ask him. I wanted to know if Kyle died instantly. I asked him if Kyle suffered any pain. I didn't want my last visual thought of my son to be one of him pinned there against the cement wall in agony and excruciating pain. He reaffirmed to me that Kyle died quickly. He told me that the train derailed and the car that Kyle was riding on overturned. Kyle was indeed pinned against the cement wall, and the rail car that was carrying coke to fuel the power plant and steel mill had overturned on top of him. He said that they had to call in some heavy equipment to set the car with the coke in it back upright and off of Kyle. That was why it took him so long to come and tell me the horrible news. He had to stay there and secure the scene until they could get Kyle out from under the rail car. But if my family wouldn't have heard from a neighbor that there was indeed an accident, I would have been home alone when the supervisor arrived to tell me about my son's death. God must have intervened and brought my sister and my nieces to me for support.

My sister Giada and I both were in shock. After the supervisor left, Giada just sat in a chair in the living room staring motionless at the floor, and I sat at the dining room table shaking and numb. I was so glad that Marie and Patrice were there to take over. The only thing that I could think of was my daughter Katerina. How could I tell her? There was no way that I could do it and Marie knew it. She called the factory where Katerina worked and talked to Katerina's supervisor. She explained what happened and that Katerina needed to come home immediately. I didn't want him to have to tell her about her brother Kyle, but he did. Katerina became so distraught that she actually had to be driven home by another employee. All I can remember is that she was screaming while she was running into the house, and she immediately went into the bathroom and threw up. She didn't even come over to me. I wanted to hug her and cry with her, but she stayed in the kitchen crying all alone. Finally, I got up and went over to her and tried to hug her, but she ran upstairs screaming and went into Kyle's room and slammed the door. I followed her up there, but when I opened the door and looked at her, she angrily screamed at me as though I had caused this horrible thing, so I turned around and went back down the stairs.

Giada called my other family members, because she was the only one that could talk to them and explain things. Luckily, she was able to reach most of them. She didn't want to tell them over the phone about Kyle, but she had no choice at the time.

When her boyfriend arrived, Katerina ran outside to greet him and the two of them held each other tightly, crying and sobbing with grief. I was so hurt that Katerina didn't say anything to me or come near me when she came in, but instead ran outside and hugged her friend for consolation. I didn't understand why she was doing this to me, and I really didn't know what I could do about it. Not only had I lost my son, but now I realized that my daughter had also turned away from me. This was almost too much for me to handle. The only thing that I could think of was what the psychologist told me a long time ago when he was working with Katerina and Kyle. I remember him telling me that a child will take their anger and frustrations out on the person that they love the most because they can rely on that person to understand them and deal with their emotions.

Her anger towards me was still difficult for me to understand, but then I also remembered two important things that my mother always told me. The first one was that God gives a person only as much pain and suffering as that person can handle. He knows a person's strength. The other thing was that there are worse things than death. But I thought to myself that enough was enough! This was way too much for me to accept! Just how strong was I supposed to be? Then I thought that maybe God was truly testing me. This was a trial that I would have to go through to prove my strength. Katerina stayed outside in the truck with her boyfriend Michael and ignored me, so I finally went back in the house.

It was then that Giada tried to coax them out of the truck. She went out and talked to them and finally, they agreed to come inside.

I suggested that we go up to Kyle's room and go through his memory box. It was a metal file box that he had under his bed that held all of his important papers and certificates and awards. We sat on his bed and cried together as we went through all of Kyle's personal things. We looked at everything in the box, the Bibles in the bookcase, the pictures on the walls, and the papers in his desk. It brought back so many memories for all of us. But there were some computer printouts that I found in his desk drawer that were questionable to me. They were articles about surrendering to God! They were something about having the most complete faith in God to guide your life, and to think and do everything in your life for God, and let him guide your path. It seemed strange to me that Kyle researched this topic and printed it out. Then I looked at the date on the printout and realized he printed it about a week before he died! What did this mean? Did this mean that he was ready to die—or that he somehow knew he was going to die? Maybe God had truly spoken to him! Maybe that was why he told me not to be sad when he died on the railroad! Maybe, that is why he was so happy that last week and at peace with himself.

I thought about how he acted lately, and the look on his face came back to me. He did seem so happy and content with his life. It just seemed so strange to me. Then another thought came back to my mind. I remembered hearing him talk out loud in his sleep just about a month earlier. He was talking so plainly and loud enough that he actually woke me up in the middle of the night. I almost thought that someone was in the room with him at the time, but then I realized, after a few moments, that he was just having a dream of some kind and talking out loud. It did seem strange though to me, because I never heard him do that kind of thing before.

I kept all of this to myself because I didn't want to stir up any trouble right then, so we went back downstairs, and Katerina went out with Michael.

Then my niece Marie suggested that we make a memory board for the funeral. She took most of the pictures home with her that night for her daughter Candy and her friend Laura, to work on it. Before the funeral, the two of them worked diligently to put it all together, but when they finally finished, it was a beautiful tribute to Kyle. They also made a video CD with background music, expressions, and thoughts about each picture.

I took Kyle's medals and certificates from singing and put them together on another board to display at the funeral home. When all of it would be finished, it would be a beautiful celebration of Kyle's life for all his friends and family to see.

My sister and brother-in-law said they would contact the funeral home for me and set up the meeting with the funeral director the next day. Then all of us needed to rest and regain some strength to continue on. My nieces said they would contact the church and make the arrangements there. My sister Giada didn't want to leave me alone, so she decided that she would stay with me, at least for a week so that I wouldn't have to be alone. I needed her support and she knew it. So the following day, Leonardo came over and brought Giada some change of clothing for her stay with me. He reassured me then that he would help me with all the financial aspects of the funeral and that I wouldn't have to worry about money. He said he would pay for all the flowers I wanted to order, and he would also pay for the food for the funeral luncheon as well. He also offered a cemetery plot for Kyle from among the plots he had secured for his family. It was in the most beautiful part of the cemetery—right next to the mausoleum and under a giant old oak tree. I agreed that it would be a wonderful final resting place for my son. I couldn't have asked for a more loving, giving, and caring brother-in-law. I hugged him and thanked him for his kindness before he left that day.

That first week, it seemed that every time I tried to relax and relieve some of my stress with a nice hot shower, I would end up crying relentlessly as the water poured over my body. Most of the time, I sobbed and gasped so much that I could hardly compose myself. Somehow I had to face it. This was not just a nightmare. It had really happened and I had to accept it. I had to go on living, but how? I wanted to die too, so that I could be with him. Katerina didn't need me or want me anymore. All that she wanted was to be with her boyfriend now. I had no one—except my sisters and their families, but I didn't want to be a burden on them. All these years, I thought that my purpose in life was to raise my two children by myself, and make sure that they would turn out to be kids that would make me proud. I especially felt that way, being a single parent. Now, all of that was over. What was my purpose in life now? I felt that I was left with nothing now and no one to love and hold on to but my dogs. Most nights, I fell asleep crying into my pillow with my dogs at my side.

The next few days were going to be a very difficult time for me. My nieces met with the sister that was temporarily in charge of my church, to plan the funeral mass. We were without a permanent priest at the time, so I knew that I would have to ask Father Joseph from another parish to say the funeral Mass for Kyle. He agreed to do it because Father Joseph really knew Kyle, especially because of my son's contemplations and struggles with becoming a priest himself. My nieces and my sister Giada handled all the necessary arrangements for the funeral luncheon, and paid for all of the food, but I had to go to the funeral home, and talk to the director to make the final arrangements. My sister and brother-in-law knew that I needed their support at the meeting, so they accompanied me. I knew I would have to sign the bill, but my brother-in-law confirmed that he would take care of it later.

I knew I had to pick out a suit and shirt and tie for Kyle, but that would be an easy task for me. I knew how much Kyle loved his suits—especially the old-fashioned ones—like the navy blue, pinstriped suit. I knew he loved his patent leather spectator shoes also, so I brought them along. The funeral director made us feel at ease, but I had to go into that other room and actually pick out the casket. I hated having to go into that room, but I spotted a beautiful one with old-fashioned engravings around the handles, and I wanted it. I didn't care what it would cost. I wanted it as long as it could be in the pewter blue color that I saw there. It was nice that they all agreed with me on my decision about it without any discussion at all. I guess everyone there wanted me to at least be happy about something that day. My sister let me order all the flowers I wanted and of course she paid for all of them. I wanted a blue and white delphinium spray for the casket. I wanted it to be different from the usual carnation sprays that most people chose. I called one of my favorite customers from the greenhouse to make the flower arrangements. I knew how talented he was as a florist and how unique his designs were. I knew it would be beautiful with Kyle's picture nested in the middle of it, because we were told that he had to have a closed casket. I was really glad of that anyway. I couldn't bear to see Kyle lying there in it. At least that way, I could remember him from his pictures instead.

After our meeting at the funeral home, my brother-in-law went up to the railroad yard to pick up Kyle's truck and get his personal belongings out of his locker. When he brought the truck over, he and I went through it and took out all of Kyle's things. It was at that time that we found a small tablet of paper under Kyle's seat that had something strange written on the first page. I read it and thought that it was quite an unusual thing for Kyle to have written down. It went like this:

"In every life, no matter how full or empty one's purse, there is tragedy. It is the one promise life always fulfills. Thus, happiness is a gift, and the trick is not to expect it, but to delight in it when it comes, and to add to other people's store of it." Charles Dickens

Again, I was very perplexed. Why did he write that down? Why was he thinking about tragedy? This was just another thing that made me question his death. That was the only thing written on that tablet of paper, and I thought it was so weird—almost as if he was expecting something to happen. That wasn't like Kyle at all to carry around a verse like that. It was almost dark and eerie, and it bothered me that we found it, but I kept it with Kyle's things, and kept my thoughts about it to myself. Hopefully, some day, I would find the answers to my questions.

When it was finally time for the initial family viewing, my nieces held my hands and walked me into the viewing room. They knew it would be hard for me to go in there at first.

When I saw the casket, I started to cry and scream out, "My baby! My baby's in that box! My baby's in that box!"

I was falling apart, and I knew I needed help. I knew that it would be very difficult for me to stand there and greet all the family and friends that would come into that room that night. I had a really bad knee that needed to be replaced, and the arthritis in my spine made it difficult for me to stand more than five minutes at a time, so I prayed really hard to the Holy Spirit and asked Him to help me stand up without pain. I put a couple of pills in my pocket just in case, and I asked for a small paper cup of water to have nearby. Soon the people would be coming in, so I had to be ready.

The first person that came in was my cousin's wife, Ruth Ann. I hadn't really known her very well, but what she had to say to me that night made a world of difference. She told me what really happened with Kyle and her daughter, Laura, during the seventieth birthday party for my Uncle Sam, a few years back. While all of the family was downstairs celebrating with my uncle, Kyle was upstairs at the piano with Laura, trying to communicate with her through music. Laura is an autistic child, and not many people have been able to get through to her at all, but Kyle did. She told me that he spent the whole evening working with Laura at the piano, getting her to smile and laugh and enjoy the music. My cousin told me that she would never forget how wonderful it was to see Kyle actually breaking through those barriers and communicating with Laura.

One by one, as friends and family came by to give me their condolences, it became easier and easier for me to stand there. The outpouring of love and support they gave me through the stories that they told me, made my burden lighter and lighter. It was as if I was floating on a cloud! I felt no pain, no hunger, and no thirst whatsoever! The words of love and the memories of Kyle that were shared with me that evening held me up and continue to sustain me to this very day. The wondrous thing is that I would never have known those stories about Kyle, if he had not died!

He made such an impression on so many people, and there were a great number of people who mourned his loss. I was able to stand there for over six hours listening to so many stories, and enjoying what I heard about him! It made me so proud of my son. There were several elementary school teachers, and the high school secretary, as well as the choral director that had special moments to relate to me. There were even people from other churches that he visited that had to tell me how Kyle impressed them. There was a young girl who told me about her experience with Kyle as her second-grade religion teacher, and another girl that told me that Kyle was her sixth-grade religion teacher. He worked with every individual, showing them how to bless themselves with the sign of the cross, at the Holy Water font, as they went into church. They told me that they would never forget about Kyle, because he showed them how much he cared for all of them.

I also talked to several of Kyle's old girlfriends. There were several of them from the high school and from the stores where he once worked. It was hard for some of them to come over to talk to me, but they did. I could tell from their expressions that Kyle meant a great deal to them. One girl still had dreams of being with him, until his tragic death stopped her hopes short. It was very difficult for her to approach me. She was so distraught. Later, I saw her weeping near the casket and talking to my sister. It was very hard for some of his friends to come near the casket, and I understood that. Some of them could only stand at the back of the room, but that was okay. I knew how they felt. There were also so many young people that had a story to relate to me about how Kyle impressed them with his knowledge of religion, or how much fun they always had with Kyle. Some of their stories were familiar to me because Kyle related a few of his escapades to me when they had occurred.

All in all, it was a very memorable and even almost enjoyable night for me, even though I was at the wake for my only son. It was truly a celebration of Kyle's life. We had his favorite music playing in the background too, and the flowers were so breathtaking. There were over one hundred arrangements around the room. Many had a toy tractor or an angel arranged among the flowers. Many of them made special keepsakes for my family and me to treasure.

The next day, the funeral Mass at our church was overflowing with people. I had to sit in the front pew by myself, although Katerina was supposed to sit with me, but she didn't want to. She sat next to her boyfriend, sobbing, while he held her in his arms again. My sisters saw that I was alone, so they both came up and sat on either side of me. It was comforting to me to have them close. There wasn't a dry eye or an empty seat in the church that day. Father Joseph said a wonderful eulogy. He commented about how Kyle always told him that he wanted a job that didn't involve manual labor. Kyle used to joke with Father Joseph and say that not having to actually do manual labor was why he wanted to become a priest! Father Joseph leaned over the casket and said to Kyle, as if he could hear him, that he was doing manual labor at the railroad, and didn't he realize it! Everyone laughed at that. Father Joseph commented too, that Kyle seemed like an eighty-year-old man in a twenty-four-year-old body. But the best thing that Father Joseph did was to sing part of the Mass in Latin as a tribute to Kyle. He knew how much Kyle wanted the Mass to still be said in Latin. But at one point while Father was singing, he gasped for breath a bit, and seemed to choke up as though he was going to cry. I felt badly for him, but I understood because Kyle was also dear to him. But later that day, at the luncheon, he confronted me about that moment. He told me that he was suddenly startled because he actually saw Kyle standing at the back of the church and smiling at him for singing the Kyrie in Latin! At first I didn't believe him, but being a priest, he must have been telling me the truth! Then I thought that maybe he was just caught up in all the emotions and stress from the day, and that he was just imagining that he saw Kyle. I really didn't grasp the meaning of it all at that time.

The resurrection choir also sang beautifully, and also did one piece in Latin for Kyle. I was pleased to hear it. Kyle's friend Ned was supposed to say a few words about Kyle there but he just couldn't do it. We had his wife read the quote from Charles Dickens that we found in Kyle's truck instead. Two of Kyle's old friends, Joseph and Brian, played their guitars and sang a song about friendship during the Mass. I don't know how they got through it because it made all of us cry again.

I chose two of my nephews and four of Kyle's friends to pall the casket at the service. They had to place the white covering over the casket during the Mass as a symbol of being a child of God—just as a white covering is placed on a child of God when they are baptized as an infant. This white cloth symbolized that from birth until death, Kyle belonged to the Lord. It was very hard for my nephew Donny to do it without crying though. He was very distraught at the service. But my littlest nephew, Drew, gave me the most support at the service, even though he was also crying. When we were supposed to walk out of the church, I had to be first to go after Kyle's casket. I was walking all alone and crying, and my little nephew saw me. He felt badly for me, so he got out of his pew and walked with me, trying to help me out. It was very touching for all to see.

Before we drove to the cemetery, Father Joseph remarked jokingly that Kyle would probably have all of the cars in the procession be held up by a train. There is a set of tracks that have to be crossed before you can drive into the cemetery, and just as Father Joseph said, the entire procession of cars had to wait for the train to go by before they could cross! We all felt that Kyle must have done that to let us know he was with us. Once we were there, we gathered inside the mausoleum at the little chapel to say our final goodbyes. My good friend Denise played "Amazing Grace" on her clarinet at the ceremony there. She played so well that most of the people actually thought it was a recording. I was really pleased that she offered to play that for me, and that she did such a fine job. Again, I was seated up front alone, so my sisters came up and sat with me.

After the ceremony there, we had to walk by his casket and say goodbye for one last time. I was numb by then, and I could hardly walk, but I stroked his casket as I passed in front of it. I didn't know how to feel as we drove back to the church for the meal. I was completely empty inside.

At the luncheon, there were over one hundred and twenty-five people served. It was so nice that the ladies of the church donated their time to serve the luncheon for us. Father Joseph even let us bring some wine into the Life Center so that we could have a tribute to Kyle with it at the meal. He also poured out a big glass of wine for my nephew Donny, even though he was too young to drink! Father Joseph felt that Donny needed it after all that he went through at the service. I almost felt like I was at a wedding reception! It was a beautiful celebration of the Mass and a delicious luncheon for Kyle's funeral.

My next hurdle was picking out a stone for Kyle's grave. I knew that it had to be done right away because it would take several weeks to be made, after I chose the actual design. My problem was that I wasn't sure what words I wanted to have engraved on the stone. I knew that I could have different things put on it that I could choose from the book at the monument company, but I wanted something more meaningful than just a cross or praying hands. For days, I kept praying to God to help me decide. I wanted it to have a verse from the Bible engraved on it, but I really didn't know where in the Bible to look.

I already went back to work after only a week because I thought it might take my mind off my troubles if I kept busy. Besides, I needed the money. I was there for just a couple of days, when my old friend Mary stopped in to see me. I didn't remember seeing her at the funeral, but that was okay. She wanted to talk to me alone. We held each other and sobbed and cried, even though I was at work. My boss understood that I was still fragile, so she let me take a break. While talking to Mary, I told her what I was looking for in the Bible for Kyle's stone and asked her if she could help me. I knew that she was a very religious person and that she recently had some special encounters with the Lord, so I was sure that she had the answers that I was looking for. She also knew that Kyle was so religious in his life, and that he wanted to be a priest at one point. She also knew that he had quite a collection of Bibles in his room. She even gave Kyle the crucifix that was on his wall over his bed. I decided to have it placed in his casket and buried with him. When I asked Mary for her help with a verse, she closed her eyes and reached out her hand as if she was looking directly into Kyle's room. She told me to look on the second shelf from the bottom, towards the left side, on his bookcase. She said that I would find a Bible bound in black leather there, and that it would be written in the New International Version. She said that I should take it off the shelf and close my eyes and open that Bible, and I would find the words that I was looking for when I opened my eyes. So when I got home, I thought it would be worth a chance to try and do as she said. I said a prayer and went directly up to his room and looked exactly where she said I was to look. I was surprised to find the exact Bible that she said I would find, just right where she said it would be! I closed my eyes and asked God to help me, and I opened the Bible, and the first words that I read were these:

"Play the harp well, sing many a song, so that you will be remembered."

Holy Bible NIV—Isaiah: Chapter 23, Verse 16

It was perfect! It was about singing and music, and it was from the Bible! I was thrilled that I found it and I called Mary and thanked her for helping me. My sister Giada and I went to the monument company the next day and placed the order for the stone. I had the verse engraved on the headstone along with a Latin cross, an antique tractor, and a Labrador hunting dog that looked similar to Kyle's dog, Sonoma. I picked a hammered pewter type edging for the stone because it reminded me of the hammered copper teakettle that my father had made. I felt that now the stone would be complete with the proper symbols on it to remember my Kyle. I was happy that the marker I chose would finalize Kyle's resting place.

Chapter Nine

Mysteries

I really had a hard time going to Kyle's gravesite at the cemetery. I didn't want to go there alone. At first, Grandma Z would drive me there, because she sensed that I longed to go there. If it weren't for her and my sister Giada, I probably wouldn't have visited Kyle's grave very much at all back then. I knew I would break down and cry, and then I would have a hard time driving home. I just couldn't go there by myself. So for the first few weeks after Kyle died, I only went there on Saturday with my sister after shopping or on Sunday with Grandma Z. The ground hadn't been smoothed over yet, and the marker wasn't put in place, but it was such a beautiful and peaceful area, so that made up for it. I was so thankful to my brother-in-law for giving Kyle such a beautiful place to be laid to rest. When you drove into the cemetery, the first thing that you saw was the stately mausoleum, directly in front. Then, if you looked slightly to the right, you would see a giant old oak tree shading the building. Kyle's grave was placed directly under that big old tree. It was so close and easy to see, even from the drive into the cemetery. Every time I walked up to the grave though, the carillon bells would play a beautiful old hymn, and I would begin to cry. I couldn't wait to see the ground smoothed over though and grass seed planted, but they wouldn't do that until the marker was in place.

Then one afternoon, I received a phone call from the cemetery services. They let me know that the marker had arrived and would be put in place that week. I was so excited to see how it turned out. I wanted to make sure that they wrote the quote from the Bible correctly, and put everything else on it that I chose. On the following Saturday, my sister and I made plans to go there and see the marker. We stopped at a department store first, and bought some silk flowers to put in the vase that came with the brass marker. I picked out a mixture of carnations, sweet pea, verbena, pansy, and delphiniums, mainly in periwinkle blue, just like the spray of delphiniums I put on his casket at the funeral home. They reminded me of his beautiful blue eyes. The flowers would be the perfect finishing touch for his resting place.

It was a beautiful marker and they completed it just as I requested. Slightly above his name, a Labrador dog was placed to the right, the brass flower vase was in the middle, and an antique tractor was placed to the left side. Directly below his name, they printed Kyle's date of birth and the date of his death. The Latin cross that I picked out was placed in the middle under the dates, and then the Bible inscription was imprinted all the way across the bottom of the marker. They finished the edges with a hammered pewter style tooling, and the whole marker was set on a slab of gray marble. It really was impressive, and now with the flowers, it was complete. I knew that many of his friends and my family would be visiting his gravesite, so I was happy that it looked so nice. I vowed to keep the vase always filled with beautiful flowers. Even if I was only allowed to put silk flowers there, they were going to look real. I was content to say a small prayer there, and then quietly go back to the car for the drive home. I knew that each time I would stop there now, it would get a little easier for me, although the pain in my heart would always be there.

The next weekend that I went there, I noticed someone had added a yellow rose to my bouquet of flowers, and placed a small cross on top of the marker. It was a little handmade cross of twigs that were tied with hemp roping. I was curious to know who went there to visit him. I thought that maybe it was one of his buddies, possibly Ned.

The following week that I visited Kyle's grave, there was another yellow rose added to the flowers, and a little note tied to the vase. It was a poem, and it was typed and laminated. It read like this:

I am not resigned to the shutting away of loving hearts in the hard ground.
So it is, and so it will be, for so it has been, time out of mind;
Into the darkness they go, the wise and the lovely,
Crowned with lilies and with laurel they go; but I am not resigned.
Lovers and thinkers, into the earth with you.
Be one with the dull, indiscriminate dust.
A fragment of what you felt, of what you knew,
A formula, a phrase remains,—but the rest is lost.
The answers quick and keen, the honest look, the laughter, the love,—
They are gone.
They are gone to feed the roses.
Elegant and curled is the blossom.
Fragrant is the blossom.
I know,
But I do not approve.
More precious was the light in your eyes than all the roses in the world.
Down, down, down into the darkness of the grave.
Gently they go, the intelligent, the witty, the brave.
I know.
But I do not approve.
And I am not resigned.

Edna St. Vincent Millay—1892-1950

There was also a medal of Jesus on a chain, draped around the flowers. I didn't know what to think now, but I was pretty sure that this time a girl must have put this poem there, but what girl? Maybe it was the girl at the funeral home that was crying, and didn't stop to talk to either Katerina or me. Now, this was starting to really make me wonder who could be doing all of this.

The next week that I went to the gravesite, another poem was attached to the flowers, along with another medal draped around the vase. This one was of the Blessed Virgin Mary. The poem went like this:

Remember me when I am gone away,
Gone far away into the silent land;
When you can no longer hold me by the hand,
Nor I half turn to go, yet turning stay.
Remember me when no more day by day
You tell me of our future that you planned.
Only remember me; you understand
It will be late to counsel then as pray.
Yet if you should forget me for a while
And afterwards remember, but do not grieve:
For if the darkness and corruption leave
A vestige of the thoughts that once I had,
Better by far you should forget and smile
Than that you should remember and be sad.

"Remember" by Christina Georgina Rossetti 1830–1894

I was really beginning to be quite bothered by all of this now. I couldn't understand, but I felt that this was another poem put there by the same girl. Whoever was doing this most likely really loved Kyle. It made me wonder if he had a secret relationship with someone that he never told anyone about. I tried to contact several of his friends and ask them if they might know who was leaving the notes and medals, but I couldn't reach anyone who could give me any answers. This really was becoming quite a mystery.

The next afternoon, I got a call from my niece, Marie, from her cell phone. She said she was at the grave with her son, Drew, to look at the notes that were left there. They had gone shopping, and decided to stop there before going home. She told me that now there was a third poem attached to the flowers! There also was a full can of Samuel Adams beer placed right on the marker! I knew that was his favorite type of beer, so I figured that a guy must have put that there. She read the poem to me over the phone, and also told me that there was a note on the back of it, written in pencil and signed! The only problem was that the signature was all smudged and illegible. She thought that the signature looked like "Karla" to her, but it was very hard to accurately decipher the name. So now I figured that there must have been two people placing things on his grave—a guy and a girl. I couldn't wait until the next afternoon, so I could go there and see the new poem and note.

This is what I found:

Of all the money ere I had, I spent it in good company,
And all the harm I've ever done, alas was done to none but me.
And all I've done for want and wit, to memory now I can't recall.
So fill me to the parting glass, goodnight and joy be with you all.

Of all the comrades ere I had, they're sorry for my going away,
And all the sweethearts ere I had, they wish me one more day to stay.
But since it falls unto my lot that I should go and you should not,
I'll gently rise and softly call, goodnight and joy be with you all.

It is taken from "The Parting Glass"—a traditional Celtic hymn.

When I turned it over, this is what the handwritten note on the back said:

Dear Kyle,

This poem is as much for me as it is for you, although I realize your journey is a lot more permanent than the one that I am about to undertake. I think of you every time a train goes by and every time I hear prayers being whispered, so you can imagine I've thought of you a lot this summer. Your death led to old friendships being renewed, and I thank you for that, but I'd gladly give it all up if it would bring you back.

If you're still out there somewhere, please continue to watch over me and bless me and I promise I'll do things that will make you proud;

and I'll keep lighting candles in your memory wherever I go.
Love, *****

At last I knew that my premonition was right! This definitely was a girl that was leaving these poems, and she certainly had feelings for my son. I was saddened though, that I couldn't make out her name from the penciled note. Marie was right. It was even hard to tell how many letters were in her name. So I had to begin another guessing game.

I finally reached some of Kyle's friends this time and asked them about the mystery name that we discovered and hoped that one of them could give me some kind of answer. I couldn't reach Ned, but I really felt that he was the one who left the wooden cross and the beer. But again, I didn't get anywhere. Everyone I contacted all said the same thing. Kyle never mentioned any particular girl to any of them. They didn't think that Kyle had been in love with any of the girls that he dated. I even went through the book that was signed by everyone from the funeral, hoping to find a name that was similar to the signature. I thought it was worth a chance to look there first, and after I read through several pages, I came across a signature that was written in a style of penmanship that looked very similar to the note. It also was just a single female name, so I felt that this could possibly be the girl. I noticed too, that her address was out of town. This might be her because the note said that she was going away. Maybe that meant that she was going to college? I looked up her address from the computer and found her phone number, but when I called it—the number was disconnected. So I thought I might try to find her last name in our county phone book. Luckily, I might stumble across her parents' phone number. I finally made a breakthrough! Her last name was so unique, that there was only one like it in our book. So I called the number and left a message on their answering machine. I also decided that I would leave a note at the grave to try to make a connection with this girl. I attached the note to a stick and set it directly in front of Kyle's marker, so that it could be seen. I said that I was Kyle's mother and I said that I wanted to talk to whomever it was that was writing the notes. I said that I wanted to share in her grief, and that maybe I could help by reminiscing about Kyle's life with her. I left my e-mail address and my cell phone number, hoping that I would hear from this mysterious girl soon. I was determined to uncover this mystery.

While talking this whole thing over with my sister the next day, she came up with another good idea. She thought that we should do another type of investigating, by starting at the restaurant that he always hung out at with his friends. Maybe the girl was one of the waitresses there? What if it was the night manager? He did mention something to me about her once. But then again, he used to put on his charm for all the girls. But I had to try to find out, so on Sunday, my sister and I stopped over there for lunch after shopping. After we ordered, Giada asked to talk to the manager. The poor young waitress thought that she did something wrong, but it wasn't about her at all. We just wanted to ask the manager if she remembered Kyle.

We wanted to know if she could tell us anything about what went on there at night while he was there with his friends. Her name was Wilma, and she had a kind, but tired expression on her face. She looked like she was in her forties. She had a round face and curly, short hair. She had a pleasant smile, and didn't mind being interrupted by our questions. She said that she was very upset when she heard about Kyle's death. Everybody there really enjoyed his company. He was a very likable guy, and the whole restaurant grieved for him. She said it was very quiet there for over a week after he died. No one wanted to say anything for fear that they would break down and cry in front of everybody. She told us how Kyle and the gang of boys and girls would all sit around there late at night and discuss the Bible over coffee. She let the gang stay there as long as they wanted because they weren't causing any trouble, and the conversations they had would get very interesting to everybody. We asked her if Kyle was serious about any of the girls that were there with them, but she told us that there wasn't any one in particular that he liked; although any of the girls would have gladly taken a shine to him, if he had been especially interested them. Most of the waitresses thought that he would be a great catch. So we were no closer in finding this girl, but we enjoyed hearing all the nice things that Wilma said about him.

After a day or two, I still hadn't heard from anyone at the phone number that I tried either, so I called it again. This time a woman answered the phone. I explained to her who I was and I asked her if she had a daughter around Kyle's age and if she knew him. To my surprise, the woman gasped on the other end of the phone, and wondered how I found her name and number! She said that it was her daughter Kihra, but she wanted to keep her feelings for Kyle to herself! The only reason her mother knew about any of this was because Kihra asked her to come along to the cemetery with her several times. She told me that Kihra was really having a hard time dealing with Kyle's death. She told me how she saw her daughter place the notes on the flowers, and then lie down on the ground next to his grave and cry her heart out! Kihra wished that I could have placed a bench next to his grave so that she could sit there and talk to Kyle. She told me she felt really bad for her daughter. She saw how saddened Kihra was and how much she was grieving, but she didn't know how to help her. She realized that she and Kyle were really close at one time. Kihra told her that she and Kyle were the best of friends since junior high school. Kihra played the cello in the orchestra, so she was around the music room and saw Kyle when he had choir practice. Kihra also was Catholic, so it was easy for the two of them to relate to each other. They had a lot in common.

Her mother related to me that the two of them carried on many conversations about religion and their favorite classical music. She said that Kihra didn't realize though, how much she cared for Kyle until he died. Kihra told her mother that she and Kyle were soul mates right from the beginning. She told her mom that she looked back through her journal, which she wrote in since she was a child, and found a lot of thoughts and memories in it about Kyle. She even wrote a paragraph or two about how she felt when she first met Kyle! She found it rather strange that she had even written about death and dying back then. She wrote that she wanted Kyle to be the first person that she met, if and when she went to heaven! She said she was about twelve when she wrote that, as if she might have had a premonition that he would die before her! It was very unsettling to her, but God must have put that thought into her head somehow.

While talking to her mother, I remembered a time when I heard Kyle and Katerina having a conversation about a girl named Kihra. It was when they both had their summer jobs at the greenhouse where I worked. It was during the summer when they were twelve and thirteen. That must have been when the two of them met. Kihra told her mother that she did have a big crush on Kyle when they were younger, but she felt that it might not be mutual, so she didn't let her feelings show. As their friendship matured, and Kyle starting seriously thinking about becoming a priest, she drifted away from him. She gave up all hope of having a serious relationship with him because of it. If she only knew that he gave up the thought of the priesthood later on, she would have told him how she felt. He probably would have felt the same way about her then. He just needed a bit more confidence in himself.

As our conversation came to a close, she told me she would let Kihra know that I was trying to contact her. Even though her daughter was away at college, she would tell her. Then it would be up to Kihra to decide if she really wanted to talk to me. I thanked her and prayed that I would hear from her soon.

A week later, I finally received an e-mail from Kihra. She said that when she came home from college on the weekend, she saw the note on the grave that I left. Her mother also told her about our conversation, and she agreed that we should meet and talk. I e-mailed her back and left my home phone number so that we could arrange a day and time to meet. But by the weekend, I hadn't received any answer, either by phone or e-mail, so I was still waiting and wondering. On Sunday though, as I was driving home from the grocery store, I spotted a small white car backing out of my driveway as I approached my home. I was about three or four houses down the street, when I passed the little white car. I noticed the girl driving it looked like she was crying as she passed my car. I realized that she probably was the girl that I wanted to meet! She must have stopped by hoping that I would be home. As soon as I got in the house, I called her mother's number again and told her how we just missed each other, so when Kirha made it back to her parents' home, her mother let her know that I called and was waiting to see her.

Finally, at 5:20 that afternoon, she was back at my door. She was a very pretty girl. She had a beautiful ivory complexion and didn't wear any make-up at all. When I saw her, I knew that she was exactly the type of girl that Kyle had always told me about. She looked like someone pure, as he used to say. She was about five feet nine inches tall, and very thin. Her hair was auburn, naturally straight, and of medium length. Her light green eyes sparkled, even through those little black rectangular glasses that she wore. She talked quietly, but very fast. I knew right away that she was very intelligent. She told me that she earned her bachelor's degree in microbiology, and was already working on her master's degree. We ended up talking and reminiscing about Kyle for over four hours! She told me that even though they were best of friends, they argued about religion all the time. She would always take the side for progress and modernization in the church, and Kyle of course, insisted on keeping the old-fashioned traditions alive. They were just the opposite in their beliefs, but she did admit to me that she harbored a long-standing crush on him. She didn't realize how much he meant to her though, and how much she loved him, until he died.

I told her everything that I could think of about his life, from the time he graduated from high school when they became distant toward each other. I told her as much as I could about his childhood, as we went through many family picture albums. I made copies of a several pictures of Kyle that she wanted, along with a few of his drawings, as mementos for her to keep. We cried together and we laughed together. We drank Kyle's favorite wine together, and we also talked about the Bible, and read some of his favorite passages together. Before she left, we hugged each other and promised to keep in touch. She said she would stop over again and see me the next time she came home again from college. It was a very memorable evening for both of us. I'm sure Kyle was right there listening to us share our stories about his life. It was comforting to both of us, and I was glad that the mystery at his gravesite finally was solved.

Chapter Ten

Passage

She was a very mysterious-looking woman to me, even though she had a very kind expression and a comforting voice when I talked to her over the phone. When I looked at her closely, I noticed that she didn't need very much make-up to accentuate her big blue eyes. They reminded me of my mother's eyes. I could tell that with her light complexion and her blond hair, that she was an Italian, or a Sicilian, from the same region that my mother was. She wore her hair and clothes in the latest fashionable styles, even though she was somewhat older than I. She had on capri slacks, and a print jacket and scarf that complemented them. Her outfit was a brightly colored, lime green nylon-silk fabric, and it went well with her coloring. She seemed camouflaged and somewhat mysterious though, and I didn't know what to expect. I had never met someone like her before. She was a psychic medium, and she was meeting with me, to try to connect with Kyle.

I never really believed in that sort of thing, but my niece contacted her as a gift for me, and arranged the meeting. I was curious and I wanted to hear her answers to some of my questions. Maybe what she would tell me was only a gimmick, but then again, maybe she did have some kind of gift, and I would find out something to bring some of my questions to a close. Her name was Abigale. A strange, old-fashioned name, but it fit her quite well. I was nervous, but anxious to hear what she would have to say.

When she first came in and sat on the love seat, Kyle's dog Sonoma jumped right in her lap, and practically mauled her with kisses in his excitement! I wanted to put the dogs outside so they wouldn't jump on her, but she told me that she loved dogs, and wanted them there. It didn't bother her at all that he was practically in her lap! My dog Simon didn't bother her at all, but Sonoma acted like he was reunited with his master! I have never seen him so excited, and he has never jumped in anyone's lap before. I was so embarrassed because of his behavior, but she was happy to connect with Kyle's dog. He wouldn't stop kissing her, and putting his front paws on her shoulders, as if to hug her; and he was smiling and wagging his tail! It was such a sight for me to see. She was talking to him and actually trying to comfort him. I started to cry because she made him so happy. Right then, I knew that she had some kind of gift. She could really connect with animals.

Before she started to talk to me though, she closed her eyes for a moment, and then she said that Kyle was connecting with her. I had an almost creepy feeling from watching her at that moment, but the first thing she told me though, was that Kyle didn't automatically go to heaven! That really surprised me. She said he had to do a lot of praying for forgiveness first, before he actually went up there! She must have meant that he was in purgatory for a while. I really wasn't sure if there was truth in what I was about to hear, but I listened intently to her anyway. Kyle told her that during those past few months that he was back home with me, he was the happiest that he had ever been in his life. She said that was the first thing that he wanted me to know. Then she said that he wanted to apologize to me! She had a curious look on her face because she didn't understand why he would say that, so she asked me if Kyle did something wrong. I smiled at her, but I didn't say anything, because I wanted to see if she really knew what he did.

But then I was amazed when she said, "What did he do? Steal something?"

My mouth dropped open! How could she have known? There was no way for her to know that he had stolen my flute and my bassoon! Only my family knew that, and Abigale didn't discuss anything about Kyle with my niece before our meeting. At that moment, I was convinced that she was actually somehow connecting with my son.

Finally, I had to tell her that she was right. I told her about the flute, the bassoon, and my diamond ring that he took from me and sold. Then she told me that he said he was deeply sorry for what he did, and he thanked me for forgiving him.

She went on to say that Kyle told her at first that he didn't know that he actually died. To him, it was like in the movie *Ghost*. He saw the train derailment, but he didn't know what actually happened. He wasn't sure where his body was. He wondered why he didn't feel any pain if he truly was in that accident. The last thing he knew was that he was riding on the outside of the train on the ladder. Kyle told her that he wasn't sure what was going on, but that an older lady and an older man came and took him by the hands up to the light.

I agreed that it must have been my mother, and Kyle's grandfather that came to meet him. They were both very close to Kyle. Naturally, she agreed. Then her eyes twinkled and she grinned delightedly, as she told me that now he was smiling and talking real fast. He was very excited and wanted to tell me everything. She seemed a little stunned when she said that he told her he was with another dog! It was a small black dog, and she was curious about that. I understood though, and I told her that it must have been Scherbrooke—Kyle's first little Scotty dog. Naturally, she said yes, that was right. Then she laughed, and told me that he really liked to drink wine and get silly! He also said that he wanted me to know that he took No-Doz pills at times, and drank a lot of coffee to stay awake, when he went on long trips with Katerina. I agreed, and I told her about the trips to Texas that he and Katerina took. I remember Katerina confessing to me back then that the No-Doz pills had him so high at one time, that he kept seeing a deer jump in front of his truck, over and over, as it crossed the road!

Then I told Abigale about the time that Kyle was at my niece Marie's home to celebrate her son Nate's birthday. He and Nate were drinking so heavily, that Kyle decided to spend the night there. He had way too much to drink, and needed to sober up, so Marie's younger son, Zeb, said that Kyle went searching for some coffee. Kyle never lived it down, when he found Marie's chocolate-covered coffee beans in her freezer instead, and ate the whole bag! Marie told me later that she was quite upset with Kyle, because that was her favorite treat. She wished that he would have eaten a whole porterhouse steak instead! She wouldn't have missed that as much as she missed the coffee beans. I went on to tell Abigale that it was the same night that Kyle went over to my sister Giada's home in the middle of the night and broke into her barn. My sister and brother-in-law were in Florida at the time. Giada's neighbors called the police because they thought a robber was stealing something there. But Kyle just wanted to play with "Unc's" tractor and start it up! His confession made a lot of sense to her then. She could tell that I worried about Kyle, because of some of the things that he did.

I was astonished again when Abigale asked me if I once had a miscarriage! She told me that Kyle was with a little cherub angel and she felt that the angel was Kyle's brother!

I confirmed to her that Kyle was supposed to be a twin, and that the other child died early in my womb, and didn't develop. That was the other placenta that I passed when I came home from the hospital after Kyle's birth. I was in awe! How could she have known that! Then she started giggling, as she told me that the older gentleman that Kyle was with was surely a stinker! Kyle told her that his grandfather really liked to tease! I laughed because that reminded me of the many times that he would slip his dried-up cud of tobacco in my palm if he could trick me into holding out my hand! He was a very fun-loving old man when I knew him. I nodded my head in agreement. She told me that Kyle felt sadness about some times in his life and how he was treated at times. She could really feel Kyle's sadness. Kyle told her that all his life he tried so hard to please some people, but he could never measure up to their expectations. At that moment, tears rolled down my cheeks. I was thoroughly convinced now that she was authentic and truly talking from her heart. She had described him perfectly. She said it was a real shame because she really enjoyed talking with Kyle. She felt that Kyle seemed like he was such a personable guy, and would have been so much fun to be with.

Then the next statement was even more remarkable. She told me that Kyle was a very *old soul*! That was just what my sister Giada and I always said about him! She said that his soul would probably never return in another life because it was so old. She could also see how talented and gifted he was in music and art. She said that when he was taken up to heaven, there was a whole band of angels singing and playing instruments! She said it was extremely beautiful. Most people have only one or two angels with them when they go up, but Kyle had a whole band!

I asked her about religion then, and she told me that Kyle had always been involved in some type of religion. He had been many preachers, teachers, priests, and ministers, in his many past lives. He told her that he held many tent revivals in the old west, and that he was a very successful preacher at one time. She said that he was always talking about religion in one form or another, and I thought to myself that this was exactly the way Kyle acted in this life! She had read him perfectly! He told her that in the past, he was active, in one way or another, during the cavalry, the Civil War, and many other historical times. I could understand now why he loved history so much, and did so well in it. I remember how sometimes, he even surprised himself about things from his past. When it came to history, he easily knew the answers because he must have already been there and been through it. This made a lot of sense to me because of his fascination with General Custer, and with naval ships like the *Monitor* and the *Merrimac*. He thrived on stories about the cavalry, Hitler and Nazi Germany, and the military in general.

Then I asked her about Katerina, and Abigale told me that she and Kyle were more than just a brother and sister. They were definitely bonded to each other and were soul mates in a past life. She told me that Katerina feels like she is also going to die soon, but that is because of her grief. She told me that Katerina would be okay, but a part of her wants to die to be with him. But yet another part of her wants to be happy and go on living, just like Kyle would want her to do. Katerina's anger made a lot of sense to me after Abigale told me that. She told me that Katerina will eventually marry her boyfriend, Michael, and they will have twins, and they will name the boy child after Kyle. She told me that Katerina is a very loving and caring person. She is also a very giving person and very sensitive. I cried even more when she told me that Kyle loved her very much. I wished that Katerina could have been there to hear what Abigale had to say. It could have helped her with her anger and her sorrow. I could understand my daughter's grief more clearly then. I was relieved to hear Abigale say that Katerina will have a long and happy life. Kyle also told Abigale that he and Katerina's boyfriend were also drinking buddies, and really enjoyed each other's company. They spent many nights talking together, out at the fire pit.

Kyle told her that he was teased a lot about a birthmark that he had and Abigale was curious to know what it was. I thought it was strange that she mentioned that, but it just helped me even more to believe in her. I told her that Kyle was missing his eyeteeth. They never developed, and it made him feel self-conscious about his smile.

The next thing she said was very hard for me to believe though. She said that because of his soul being so old, at one time he actually walked the Apian Way with Jesus, and at another time he even painted with Michelangelo and other masters! She told me that he was very artistic and very musical, but he also loved old tractors and old steam locomotives. He was happiest being on the trains and he loved his job. He kept to himself at work and he was a free spirit. He loved working outside, riding on the trains, and feeling the wind on his face. When she said that, I gasped! That was exactly how he always said it to me! I remember him telling me about the time he was riding on the train at night and saw the stars as he was looking up. He was so happy then. I remember how he told me that he saw heaven through the stars. I started to cry again. I missed him so much right then. My heart was aching.

I didn't even ask her, but Abigale told me that Kyle loved me very much and he wanted me to know that he would never commit suicide! She said that he was very adamant about telling me that. Then I remembered my doubting him, and I was sorry for thinking that way about him. I should have known that he would never do such a terrible thing. He was too religious. He told her he knew he was going to die on the railroad though, but he didn't know how or when.

He told her that he felt I was a very good mother to him and he especially liked that I never judged him. He liked that I just let him do his own thing—what he enjoyed most in life.

He told her how proud he was of me. Abigale also told me that I would have a long life, that I would always be safe, and that I would always have a purpose in life.

I asked her about Kyle's best friend Ned next. She told me that Ned and Kyle were so close that they were bonded at the hip! They did everything together. She said that Ned didn't know how to react to Kyle's death and he almost tried to commit suicide. He never lost anybody close to him before, and he had a lot of difficulty dealing with it. That is probably why I wasn't able to contact Ned.

I asked her about my sister Giada next. She told me that Giada will be fine and that she will have a long life. She said that her cancer will not come back. I was extremely relieved to hear that.

Next, she told me that Kyle really loved the water! That was something that I could hardly believe because Kyle never wanted to go swimming. I didn't understand why she said that, until I asked Katerina about it the next time I saw her. My daughter told me later that Kyle truly enjoyed swimming when they were on the beach in Houston. Katerina told me that Kyle actually took his shirt off and swam in the ocean! He loved it very much but he got terribly sunburnt from it, and Katerina had to put aloe on his back to help it heal. He was really burnt, but she didn't let him know just how bad it actually was.

Abigale told me that Kyle said he would always be with us in our dreams. He told her that the answers to the questions we have would be in the first thoughts that will come into our minds. She also said that he would be messing with the lights! That would be the way that we would know he was near us.

I laughed when she told me that my sister Giada and I both have some psychic ability. We just haven't developed it yet. That is probably why I have felt his presence around me at times, and Giada also has had some premonitions.

After the session with Abigale was over, I showed her some of Kyle's drawings and the pictures that I had of him. As she was leaving, she said that she wished she could have met him when he was alive. He really impressed her as being such a wonderful guy, and she really enjoyed talking to him and also to me. I thanked her, and she gave me a big hug before she left.

Chapter Eleven

Visions

I knew that going back to work after only a week was going to be difficult, but I hoped that it would take my mind off of my grief. Keeping myself busy on other things would give me the escape that I needed. But sometimes it didn't quite work that way. It seemed that every day I would think of Kyle from the moment I woke up until the time that I went to back to sleep, but especially when I got into the car to drive to and from work. I cried uncontrollably during most of my drive, on so many days. I was so sad, even though Kyle had asked me not to be. How could I *not* be sad? What was there to be happy about anymore? I also was still very angry with the Lord for taking my son away from me. I hadn't really doubted my faith, but I also hadn't really practiced it wholeheartedly either. For several years, I gave up on going to church or even praying at all. But when my children were younger, I made it a practice to go to church every week, even though I really didn't feel any different because of it. Back then, I wanted to instill good religious practices in them, and I guess it worked on Kyle, but not necessarily on Katerina.

I had the most difficulty controlling my emotions when I had to drive through the wooded area before the railroad tracks, on the country road by the greenhouse. The quiet, secluded beauty of the trees and foliage there reminded me of Heaven when I looked up through them at the light as I drove. It seemed odd, but I never forgot that it was there, just before the tracks, that I used to see the same vision over and over. It was of a man standing in the middle of the road, wearing a black trench coat, with his arms outstretched. I could never see his face, so I wasn't sure who it was or why I saw him standing there. I never really understood why—until Kyle died. Then it all came back to me and made some sense. It must have been some sort of warning that God was giving me, about Kyle dying on the railroad. This went on for close to a year, but then after he died, I looked for the man in the same spot in the woods every day, but I never saw him again. For several weeks, I guess I was either in a daze or just numb from my loss. Still though, I went on through life, carrying my struggle inside.

On my desk pad at work was a really nice picture of Kyle that my nieces missed when they went there to collect pictures of Kyle for the funeral. I thought now, that I would take that picture to the store and have it enlarged and make several copies of it for my family. I knew how to use the photo machine at the store by myself because I knew the code without the help of a sales associate, so I went there directly after work one day. When I arrived, there was a young woman at the copy machine before me, making pictures of her son. It must have been in God's plan for me to be there, because her son had also just died. He was only eighteen and died in his sleep from an aneurysm. The poor woman was so distraught because she felt that she somehow could have prevented his death. Her son told her that night, that he had a severe headache, dizziness, and wanted to see a doctor, so she had planned to make an appointment for him in the morning. But then it was too late. I hugged her as she sobbed and cried while telling me her story. Then I tried to comfort her and also tell her about my son's tragic death, so that we could grieve together. I think that by the time she finished with her pictures, she felt a little better because of our sharing.

Then it was my turn to make some copies. I had no trouble making the first set of pictures. The touch screen was easy to manipulate for me. But when I tried to make the second set of pictures, I couldn't get the screen to respond to my touch at all. I became very frustrated and I almost started to cry because there was no one around to help me. I knew the girl who normally worked in that department, but she wasn't there. Maybe her shift hadn't started yet, or maybe she had already gone home. My frustrations were getting the most of me by then, and I really broke down. It was then that I asked God for help. I asked Him to please bring Ruby there to help me. I turned around and looked for her twice while I was praying to God to bring her to me, but still she wasn't there. But on the third time that I turned around, there she was! I couldn't believe it! She was all dressed up and not there to work at all! She was actually there to make copies of a picture of her father-in-law because he had also just passed away! She helped me with my pictures after I told her about Kyle, and then she made her pictures and left. It was so strange!

I smiled and said to myself, "Praise God! Thank you, God, for sending her to me!"

This definitely was not just a coincidence! I could feel the Lord's presence around me, and I knew that he was guiding me. It was such a strange feeling at first, but I could feel some comfort, and a little less anger at God for what He did for me.

The following week while I was at work, I received a call from my old friend Denise. She was crying and asking for my help. She needed to have someone to console her because her husband Tim had gone into a seizure and had a stroke! She was alone because her family lived three hours away. She had to put Tim in a nursing home because he lost his speech and was incontinent and couldn't walk or take care of himself. I knew that he had been ill for many years, and was in and out of the hospital, but I didn't know how serious his illness had become. He suffered from brain tumors caused by a rare blood disease that made his blood either too thick or too thin at times. Over the years, he went through several operations to try to remove the tumors, but without much success. He had many grand mal seizures, but this time was the worst of all. I felt badly for her, and wanted to help her in any way that I could because she was there for me all through Kyle's funeral.

I went with her to the nursing home the next afternoon to visit Tim. On the way there, we had to stop at a railroad crossing, for a train to go by, but only one little engine passed by us heading west. I thought that was kind of peculiar. I looked at her and said, "Kyle must have planned that to say hello to us."

I felt that he was with me, but she didn't have anything to say about it. She just listened with a grin on her face.

As we drove, she warned me that Tim probably wouldn't respond to me at all because of the severity of his stroke, but I wanted to try to talk to him anyway.

When I went in, I approached his bed, and quietly said, "Hello, Tim. How are you?" even though I knew I wouldn't get a response.

I told him who I was, and I hoped that he would remember me somehow. Then I told him about Kyle's death and I reminisced about the fun times that Kyle and Katerina had spent with him when they were little. I reminded him of his role as the Big Yellow Bird, and how much all the children adored him, but he just stared at me with an empty expression. I don't think he even knew I was in the room.

After about half an hour, we decided to leave. Denise said that she was working his arms and legs every day and trying to get him to talk and to respond to her voice. But I could see that no one was getting through to him anymore. It was very hard for her to deal with all of this. She felt that he was going to get better and was going to be able to come home with her in a week or two, but I knew that there was no way that she could take care of him now. I tried to talk to her about it in the hallway outside of his room, before we went home, but then something amazing happened. I actually heard Tim speak! He was clearly calling Kyle's name!

I looked at Denise with amazement and said, "Did you hear that? Did you hear Tim say Kyle?"

She said she did hear something, but she tried to pass it off as some kind of electron backfire in his head causing a belated muscle response to verbalize involuntarily, but I knew better. I knew Kyle was in the room with him and communicating with him somehow. It was a gift from Heaven because Tim could not speak at all! He had only been mumbling ever since his stroke, but this was a very clear response! He clearly and loudly said Kyle's name!

Again, I felt that God had intervened and was trying to show me His presence. Little by little, my anger was diminishing into joy from His love.

On the way back home, we had to stop at the same railroad crossing again. It was amazing to me, because the same little engine crossed in front of us again, but was heading east this time! I truly felt that this was in no way just a coincidence. That railroad crossing hardly ever had a train traveling on it, and we never saw just a single engine go by on any given day! How could that little engine pass by us twice in the same day? That was incredible! Kyle had to be trying to reach us, but Denise still acted like she didn't believe any part of it at all. She told me that her feelings were, that when someone dies, they just die. They are gone. She didn't believe that they could go to Heaven or to hell or to anywhere. I just listened to her and didn't say any more about religion to her. It was no use. She made me so nervous when she started telling me her views on religion, because she would raise her voice to the point that I felt that she was yelling at me, and I didn't want to get her provoked again.

A week later Denise phoned me to tell me that Tim finally died in his sleep. She was crying on the other end when she told me that she wasn't going to have any funeral service for him at all. She already had his body cremated and brought his remains home in a box. She planned to scatter them around at all the places that he loved in his life.

I tried to talk to her about religion and God again, especially since Tim was a Catholic, but she didn't want to hear about it anymore. I felt badly that he didn't have any funeral service, but she became even more distant to me then. I learned weeks later that Denise turned away from God altogether, and decided to become an atheist! That is why she couldn't accept Tim's response to Kyle, or have a funeral service for him. It made it difficult for me to talk to her at times.

As I continued to go through the daily grind at work, there were times that little things would happen to me that would ease my pain somewhat. One day while I was walking out to the mailbox at work, I asked God to let me know and see that Kyle would still be with me. I guess I still wanted to be shown because my belief was still questionable. I could release my sadness by crying as soon as I walked out of the building, and away from people. I felt the sun shining on my face and the warmth from it on my shoulders, as I looked down and saw my shadow on the ground where I walked. A feeling of comfort came over me, and a warmth came from within my heart. It was such a strange feeling to me, but it actually felt like someone was truly walking alongside of me! I looked down at my shadow as I walked and hoped that I could see another shadow walking beside mine, but I didn't. Even though I didn't see him, I felt his presence next to me. It was comforting to me and some of my anger and sadness went away again that day.

Another strange thing happened one day on my way to work, shortly after Kyle died. I had to stop at the tracks on the road before the greenhouse, because I heard the whistle of a train coming. I have never seen a train like this one before and I have never seen one like this since then either. Except for the engine, the entire train was made up of gondola cars that said "Coke Express" on them. They were not rusted over, but instead were very new looking and painted a steel gray color. I spotted the little ladder that ran up the side of them, and immediately I knew that this was the type of gondola car that Kyle worked on and that fell over on him and killed him. It was an eerie feeling to see such a train pass in front of me. It was even stranger though, when Katerina called me later from town that same day, to tell me about an unusual train that she had to stop for. When she described it, I knew that it had to have been that very same train!

I wasn't the only one that was having strange things happen to them. Within the first couple of weeks after Kyle was gone, my niece Rochelle and her husband both felt that Kyle was connecting with them just about every day. On their way to and from work, they had to cross a set of railroad tracks that seemed to be playing tricks on both of them. Rochelle said that one day while she had stopped at the tracks before crossing, she saw a headlight of a train coming towards her about a quarter mile down the track. By habit, she turned her head to look in the other direction down the tracks, but when she looked back again, there wasn't a train there at all! She swore that she saw a train coming at first, but then it was gone! Immediately, she thought of Kyle. Her husband told her that just about every day within those first few weeks, something strange also would happen to him at the tracks. He would have to stop there, because the crossing gates would be down and he swore he could hear the whistle of a train coming. But a few moments later, the gates would go up and the tracks would be clear! Rochelle told him that it also happened to her in the same way. The two of them were convinced that Kyle was playing tricks on them at those tracks.

The whistle of a train also seemed to stop my niece Patrice and her boyfriend, every time they would have a serious discussion in her kitchen. That was where she put the picture of Kyle that I gave her. She told me that just about every time she would get upset, she would hear a train whistle blow and she would know that Kyle was there listening to them. It always made them smile and forget about their problems for the moment. She remembered how much Kyle wanted her to be happy and enjoy life.

My niece Marie also told me that the night after Kyle died, she felt his presence in her bedroom. She was sleeping soundly, but was awakened by a very bright light in her bedroom. It was as though the headlights from a car were coming into her bedroom window, but that would be impossible unless the car was heading directly across her side lawn! She never saw such a light as bright as that shining into her window before. Marie's home is also out in the country where there are no streetlights, so she couldn't mistake the light she saw for a street lamp. She sat up in her bed and looked around the room, but couldn't see anything more, but she felt a warmth coming from within her body, from her waist up and through her head and face. She knew it had to be Kyle greeting her. She smiled and went back to sleep.

When she told me her story, she also told me three days before he died that she had another strange thing happen. A thought had passed through her mind that she had to clean her house before the funeral! Then she thought to herself—what funeral? She didn't say anything to anybody about her thought though, but after Kyle died, it frightened her somewhat when she realized that she must have had the premonition of a funeral, but never expected it to be for Kyle!

My daughter Katerina was still distant to me somewhat even though she did speak to me when I called her. I could still feel her anger. I wanted to be able to see her and sit down and talk to her. I wanted to be close to her again, especially since I had no one else, but I didn't know how I could get her to love me again. I guess she was the reason that I started praying again. I made it a point to say a little prayer every day when I got into my car to drive to work. It wasn't much, because I was still somewhat angry with God, but I knew that I needed His help. I read somewhere that I should be thankful that God *gave* me my son for the twenty-four years that I had him. That statement was hard for me to accept at first, because I always thought that Kyle was all mine. But when I looked at the big picture in life, I realized that he belonged to God first and God was just *lending* him to me for a while. He was a child of God first—then a child of mine. I realized that I also should feel the same way about Katerina. So as hard as it was for me to say at first, I thanked God for what He had given me rather than resented Him for what I had lost. I actually typed up a little prayer and laminated it and taped it to the dashboard of my car so that I would see it and make myself read it every day. Little by little, it became easier to say as my heart softened. I began to pray daily for the Holy Spirit to come into my heart and into Katerina's heart as well. Over several weeks, I did notice a gradual change in her and in myself daily, as I continued to pray.

On one early Sunday morning, I was upstairs on the computer making copies of some of Kyle's pictures. I knew that Katerina didn't have any copies of most of them, so I thought of a plan to see her. I figured that I might be able to entice her to stop over if I had some pictures of Kyle to give her. But another strange thing happened. Just as I finished printing the pictures, the phone rang. It was Katerina and she was crying!

Sobbing quietly, she said, "Mom?"

I calmly said, "Yes, Katerina."

She replied in a tearful voice, "Mom, could you make me some more pictures of Kyle? My dogs chewed up the pictures that I had of him on the coffee table."

I was stunned! I paused for a moment and caught my breath, and then I replied, "I am printing some off for you right now! Please come over here right away. I want to hug you!"

She said "Okay" softly, and hung up the phone.

I knew that this was God helping me get close to my daughter again! This just couldn't have been a coincidence! When she walked in the door, I put my arms around her and gave her a big hug and I told her how much I loved her. I told her that we needed each other now that Kyle was gone. She cried and hugged me back, and I kissed her on the cheek. Just then, my sister Giada surprised us with a visit, and came in. She greeted Katerina and hugged and kissed her also. Katerina had been distant to her as well, so this was a perfect chance for them to make amends. I thanked God for answering my prayers. After that, we all went outside and sat on the porch and talked for a while. I had my daughter back, and I thanked God over and over again for bringing her back to me.

She called me a couple days later to tell me that she recently had a dream about Kyle. She wasn't really sure if it was a dream or if he really visited her in the night. She told me that Kyle talked to her just as though he was still alive. He told her that he would come to visit her and everyone in our family every day. He told her that he would still be with her always. He even said he visited and played with his dogs every day too. She thought it was funny, because he told her he could only stay for ten minutes because he had to go to work! She told me that she felt a little more at peace after she talked to him.

Katerina's boyfriend also told me about a dream he had right after Kyle died. He told me that his dream was at the funeral home in front of Kyle's casket. In his dream, the casket was open and Kyle opened his eyes and started talking to him. He dreamt that he nudged Katerina to see if she also saw Kyle awake and talking in the casket. But she was not paying any attention to him or to Kyle. He said that he shouted at everyone to look at Kyle talking, but no one heard him. Kyle said to him that he was happy and that he was in Heaven and that it was beautiful up there. He said that he was killed instantly and that it didn't hurt him at all. He said that the tracks were faulty and that the dogs, which are the mechanical devices that lift a rail car up to dump the coke, were up instead of down, and that caused the derailment. In his dream, Kyle asked him to make sure that I take good care of his dog Sonoma, and not to get rid of him. Kyle told him that he was glad that he was the one that died and not Katerina. He wouldn't have been able to deal with her death. He said he loves her very much. He said that he is watching over all of us, and protecting us from harm. He is happy in Heaven and he is with God. He said he is at peace and he will see us in our dreams.

When Katerina heard that, she was more relieved and I could see her anger passing away again. I think she felt it even more believable because it was coming from her boyfriend. I was glad to hear his dream as well. It was comforting for all of us to hear.

My sister Giada also had a premonition before Kyle died, but she didn't tell anyone about it until after he was gone. At the time, she felt that it was such a bad thought, that she wanted to put it out of her mind. It was when she was coming out of her surgery on the fifth of May. She was still groggy from the anesthetic, but a thought came into her head that there was going to be an accident at Kyle's work and that he would be killed. After it really came true, she felt terrible that she hadn't warned Kyle about it. But then again, knowing Kyle, he probably would have just laughed it off anyway.

My niece's daughter, Connie, had an experience one afternoon, where she also felt that Kyle was with her. She was very upset and crying over an argument that she had with her dad about the car that he bought her. Her dad was going to take it away from her if she didn't go to the soccer tournament that she was supposed to play in. She was so overwhelmed at the time, because she was trying to juggle her schoolwork, her job at the pizza parlor, and being on the soccer team; so at the last moment, she felt it was impossible to go to the tournament. But her dad demanded that she go, or he would take the car away from her. She was crying and sobbing up in her room because of it. While sitting on her bed, she suddenly felt a presence in her room. She said that a warm feeling came over her and she could feel that Kyle was sitting right next to her on her bed. His presence frightened her so much that she ran out of the room. But after she calmed down, she wished that she had stayed there, because she realized that Kyle was only trying to comfort her.

On a visit from my sister Giada and brother-in-law Leonardo one day, Kyle let us know he was present again. My sister had insisted that I get new living room furniture to try to cheer me up. She took me shopping, and Leonardo and Marie painted the room before the furniture arrived. When everything was all arranged, and the room was complete, they stopped over to see how it looked. Leonardo sat in the chair next to the lamp by the window and Giada sat on the recliner. I was across the room talking to them, when I noticed the lamp by Leonardo kept going on and off. I watched it for several minutes before I said anything to them. It was strange because the light was not flickering. It would stay on for at least a minute or two, and then it would go off for about thirty seconds or more, and then come back on again. I think that is why it wasn't noticeable to them.

When I mentioned it to them, they were silent as they watched the light turn on and off, over and over again. I told them that I thought it was Kyle trying to say hello to them; but they didn't know what to think, and they didn't say anything more about it. After they left, the lamp stopped working altogether. I thought it was the bulb, so I replaced it, but it still didn't work. I finally had to replace the lamp.

There was one night that Katerina decided to spend the night with me, because she had an argument with her boyfriend, and wanted to have some time alone. I liked the idea of having her back home with me anyway, but during the night, another strange thing happened. Katerina was sound asleep in her bedroom and I had the door closed to my room. The dogs were happy to have her back, so they slept in her bedroom. But late that night, I awoke from the smell of Kyle's fresh pipe tobacco. My room was filled with the aroma of the fresh, sweet, cherry vanilla tobacco! Kyle never smoked his pipe in front of me because he knew I couldn't tolerate the smoke, but I liked the smell of the fresh tobacco in his pipe. I sat up in bed and I continued to smell the tobacco! I was not asleep and I was not dreaming. I was wide-awake. I looked around the room for his presence, but I couldn't see anything because I didn't have my glasses on and the room was very dark. I called out to him softly and told him that I knew he was with me, and I wasn't afraid. It was a good feeling, and very comforting to me to know that he was near. In the morning, I asked Katerina if anything strange happened to her overnight, but she said she slept so soundly and that she couldn't really remember anything.

There was another time later on, that Katerina woke me up late at night because she saw something strange in her apartment. She told me that it was an image of a man, who she thought was Kyle, looking at her through her front window. It scared her at first, but then she felt sure that it was Kyle. Within a few more days, she woke me up again in the middle of the night, but this time she was screaming. She was hysterical because she said she saw him in her bedroom! She said that she woke up from a sound sleep, and as she rolled over in her bed, there he was! She could see the entire image of Kyle, through the moonlight, walking directly past her door that led to her bathroom. She was shaking and crying and extremely frightened, so I tried to console her and help her pray so that she wouldn't be afraid—especially if it was her brother. I told her that he wasn't going to harm her. He was just letting her see that he was still with her. I was amazed and a little frightened myself, but I didn't want her to know that. I fell back to sleep by praying to my guardian angel to also protect me. It was after that episode that I realized that I should try to go back to church.

The next day, Katerina and her boyfriend stopped over to see the new living room furniture. The three of us were sitting in there talking and Katerina mentioned again how she saw Kyle in her bedroom. I listened to her explain it again, but she seemed hesitant that it might not be Kyle—but a real live man that might have broken into her apartment. For some reason, I questioned her feelings again, and asked her if she thought it might be the devil. What happened next really startled all three of us. As soon as the word "devil" came out of my mouth, the angel statue on that same table with the lamp fell right over! Our mouths dropped open! We all looked at each other in shock!

Katerina shockingly kept saying "Oh, my God! Oh, my God!"

I couldn't say anything, and neither could her boyfriend. We all just sat there with our mouths open in amazement!

That next Sunday, I got ready to go to church, but I wasn't really even sure what time the Masses were scheduled. I suppose I didn't exactly care either. I thought that I would just try to go—even if I went in late, at least I would be going. When I pulled into the parking lot, I saw that it was pretty full, so I knew that the Mass had already started.

I drove to the place where I usually parked, figuring that it would be taken, but hoping that it was empty. But when I got there, I couldn't believe it! That spot was the only space in the whole parking lot that was empty! I was amazed, and thankful to park there.

I always used to go into the church by the side door, but since the Mass had already begun, I walked all the way around to the front door to enter. I didn't want anybody see me coming in late. The church was completely full when I went in, and there were even people standing in the back. With my bad leg and back, I knew that I couldn't stand through the whole Mass, so I looked for a seat in the back few pews by the side aisle. Again, I was surprised to see that there was one seat empty at the very end of the third pew from the back! I quickly knelt down in it and started to pray. First I thanked God for making it easy for me to come back to church, and then I prayed real hard and asked Him to give me strength and guidance.

I went through the entire Mass without a tear falling—that is until the very end. As the people were walking out of the church, I saw two of my cousins. Naturally, they came over to greet me and give me a gentle hug. They were glad to see that I had come back to church. I started to feel as if I was going to cry, so I tried very hard to hold it back. But before I could leave, another friend of mine came over when she saw me. She actually is a close friend of my niece Marie, and also a music therapist/psychologist as well. I thought she would just say hello and give me a hug, but instead she sat down beside me and put her arm around my shoulder. She knew how much I was hurting and she wanted to comfort me. Of course, I broke down and began to cry and sob to the point that I could hardly catch my breath. I guess I needed a good cry at that point, and I actually didn't care who saw me like that anymore. I finally had made it back to church and I felt so bad for all the times that I had missed. Sometimes the easiest little things in life are the hardest things to do.

On another Sunday, my neighbor Grandma Z and I met up with an older friend of hers, as we were walking up the sidewalk to church. The two of them were talking and walking slowly, side by side, and I didn't mind walking slowly behind them, because of my bad knee. Suddenly,

I felt that there was a person behind me that wanted to pass, because he was walking much faster than the three of us. I felt that he almost stepped on the heel of my shoe, because he was walking so close behind me. So I stopped and turned around to tell him that he could just go around us. But the strangest thing was that no one was behind us at all! There wasn't a single other person around—even in the parking lot or on the sidewalk!

I laughed to myself and thought that it must have been Kyle trying to hurry me into church.

Some things in life though, will always make me sad about Kyle. That is inevitable. One thing that Kyle and I alone shared, in our family, was the love for the music of Mozart. Between the two of us, we had just about every recording of his music that we could find. Although there were many other composers that he favored, he knew that above them all, Mozart was my favorite. When Kyle was at home, I sometimes would hear him singing something from the opera *The Magic Flute* just for me to hear. He never sang alone to anyone other than me, but he had such a beautiful voice. I think he was either embarrassed, or too shy, to sing by himself; although performing on stage with the choir was easy for him. He had promised me that one day, he would take me to see that opera, when it would be performed in our area. We both loved it very much. Kyle especially loved the baritone arias sung by the character Sarastro in the story. They were easy for him to sing along with, because they were all in his vocal range. Sadly though, we never got to actually see that opera performed. So after he died, I ordered a CD of it, performed in Austria on authentic period instruments, making it as original a performance as possible. I watched it all by myself at home alone one night. I shouldn't have, because I knew I was going to cry all through it, but I longed to hear Kyle singing to me again. This would be the closest way for me to remember his voice, so I didn't care how sad it would make me feel. It was a bittersweet memory, and I cried all the way through those baritone arias, but I had Kyle's voice back in my head again, and that was comforting to me.

Still though, there were many hard times where I was so sad and missed Kyle so much. One of those times, I was driving to work, and crying real hard while I was listening to my favorite classical music station. I was upset anyway, because I had to go into work on that day because it was the Fourth of July. I should have been home sitting outside in the sun on such a beautiful day, but it was my turn to work the holiday. I thought that if they would play some Mozart on the radio, it might make me feel a little better, but the station was playing some modern piece instead. But just at that moment, the announcer said that she was going to play the opera *The Magic Flute* by Mozart! So through my sobs and wails of tears, I actually started laughing! It was as though Kyle was sitting there, right next to me and trying to comfort me by saying, "Here, Mom, listen to this! It's your favorite! Please don't cry!"

I was suddenly crying and laughing at the same time! It was so strange, that I was stunned! That station would never play *The Magic Flute* opera on the Fourth of July? That opera was usually only played during the Christmas holidays because of its magical and fantasy-like libretto. I really felt that Kyle was sitting right next to me there—trying to take away my sadness that day.

By the end of that first month, Katerina told me that she had another strange incident happen to her about Kyle. She was at the factory where she worked, and she accidentally dropped a part that she was working with. She said that when she bent down to pick up the part and then stand up again, Kyle was standing directly in front of her! She froze in her spot in shock, but when she blinked, his image went away. This time, she wasn't scared at all. She felt really good that she had seen him. It gave her comfort to really believe that he was with her wherever she was.

Most of the time, going through the daily routine at work and at home kept my mind off of my grief. But there were times when I let my worries get the best of me. I was struggling so much to understand the purpose of it all. It really bothered me that Kyle knew he was going to die. It made me wonder, and question the whole accident. What if someone purposely caused the derailment because they wanted to kill my son? There was no possible way that Kyle could have committed suicide. He couldn't have caused the derailment if he was hanging on to a car as it rode down the tracks. So even if it was God's plan to take Kyle at that time, was it somehow a way to uncover the safety problems at that railroad? If it really was about the safety problems, then how was I going to get them to fix it? Was that the purpose for Kyle's death?

My mind went over and over this, to the point sometimes, that I thought my worries and anxieties would get the best of me. But then something very strange and wonderful happened to me. While I was carrying a load of laundry down the stairs, and worrying about all of this, God actually spoke to me! Just as I reached the bottom step, with my arms full of laundry, a very loud and deep voice echoed in my head. God called me by a very peculiar name, but I knew that it was me that He was speaking to, so I stopped immediately in my tracks and listened as God spoke.

He called me by this name and said, "Do not worry! Everything will be all right!"

I tried to ask Him something more about it, but there was no answer. God had left my mind just as quickly as He had entered it. There was no more to say and I felt then that I was not to question Him again. For a few minutes, I actually didn't even realize what had just happened to me. I guess I actually was in shock. God himself—took the time to stop and speak to me? How wonderful!

All I could think of now, was to keep saying "Let go, let God!" over and over in my head. For weeks and weeks, I kept saying that until I finally stopped worrying about it altogether.

During this same time of struggling and questioning, I continued to go to church and pray. On one Sunday when I was having a real hard time with my sadness, God came to help me again. I was kneeling right after communion and praying very hard for God to help me with my grief, when I happened to turn my head and look toward the side altar. There, before my eyes, was the image of my son Kyle—kneeling and praying! My eyes opened wide and my mouth dropped, as I took a deep breath and froze my gaze upon him. I clearly saw my son kneeling at the side altar, with his hands in prayer, and his gaze upon Jesus on the crucifix above the altar! I couldn't believe what was happening! I could see him, but I could also see through him. It was just how you would see a ghost if you were watching him on the television. But I will never forget the image that I saw of my son. He had on a red plaid flannel shirt and dark-colored blue jeans. His hair was cut very short, and his beard was trimmed close to his face. He even had on a pair of work boots! He was clearly kneeling there for at least five or ten seconds, before I turned my head to Grandma Z to ask her if she saw him there like I did. But when I turned my head back to gaze at him, he was gone. It was truly amazing!

God gave me these two special gifts that most people will never, ever get. The gift of God's voice speaking to me in my head and the gift of seeing my son again, after his death, are truly something very, very special. It was so wonderful to see Kyle's beautiful face again and his body whole—especially after the accident and having a closed casket at the funeral. I know that God did this for me because I kept my faith in Him and I offered up my worries to Him. I read somewhere that if you take one step toward God—He will run toward you two. I "Let go and let God," and I was rewarded.

Chapter Twelve

Beliefs

I had an awful dream several months after Kyle died. I guess I was still somewhat in limbo with my feelings. At times, I was feeling the fear of being alone, and questioning the reason for his death, or fantasizing that I would wake up someday and he would still be alive and be here with me. That is probably why I had this terrible nightmare. I dreamt that I was sleeping comfortably in my own bed, and Katerina was sleeping next to me. It must have been because she was scared and needed comforting also. In the dream, she woke me up because she felt a presence in the room and was scared. She didn't know what it was. I sat up and looked through the darkness toward the door, but I didn't have my glasses on so I couldn't really see much of anything at all. I thought that it might be Kyle coming again to see us in the darkness. But then I noticed the black, billowing smog creeping up from under the door. I sensed that it was evil and that it was creeping toward my bed. I grabbed my daughter in the dream and tried to protect her and myself from the evil presence. Then I actually woke myself up from the dream because I was pleading to God for His help. I started to pray for His protection and to take my fears away. Eventually, I fell back to sleep singing one of my favorite hymns that I remembered from church. It is the hymn called "Be Not Afraid."

When I woke up the next morning, I decided that I needed to increase my faith. I was ready to start reading and studying the Bible.

I remembered that Kyle collected many different versions of the Bible in his room, and I knew that he read through many of them, but I also found out that he had read the New American Bible version from cover to cover, because his copy was highlighted all the way through. So I purchased a copy of that version for myself. I didn't know if there were any actual study groups at our church at that time, but I wanted to find out. I asked my neighbor, Grandma Z, if she knew of any, and if she would go with me to a Bible study, if we could find one. I knew that my sister Tina went to a Bible study at her church, and I saw how spiritual she had become from it. Grandma Z was delighted at the thought of attending a study group with me, so she looked into it right away. The next day, we were in luck, because she found out that there was a special outdoor Bible study meeting that we could attend that very same night. I really didn't know what to expect, but after attending it, I was thirsting for more. We found out that there were several different meetings going on weekly at our church, so we made a commitment to each other that we would attend at least one of the meetings a week. So after a couple of weeks of Bible class, we both were convinced that it was making quite a difference in our lives. The people that we met there were very kind, understanding and patient with our lack of knowledge of the Bible. They were always ready to help us understand and find the meaning in the scriptures. Through their help, we both could see how the scriptures could relate to us in our everyday lives.

Through the wonderful friendships that developed from the Bible study, we became involved in helping our church and our community with the soup luncheons held there. Most of the members of the Bible class were already in charge of cooking and serving these meals, so we also felt that we needed to help them. It is something that has given both of us a wonderful feeling of satisfaction, when helping and giving to others. I know now that, little by little, my neighbor and I are growing in our faith. The more that I go to church now, the more that I understand, and feel the Holy Spirit coming to me, especially each time I go to communion. It reminds me also, of what Kyle said to me after he was confirmed—when he felt the Holy Spirit come upon him. I know that this was one of the things that God wanted me to learn from

Kyle's death. Growing in my faith has helped me to understand why Kyle was so happy and fulfilled with his life before he died. He had made a commitment and surrendered himself to God.

I have also learned from Kyle's death, that he isn't really gone from my life. I know he has tried to connect with me and with others in my family, many times. My whole family is convinced from all that has happened that Kyle is near us all the time. They in turn, have increased their faith and become closer to God, because of Kyle's death. It is comforting to us and it has softened our grief.

There also was another experience that I had, that helped to confirm this feeling in me. I was on my way to work one morning early, and as I turned onto the dirt road, I noticed something moving close to the road in the distance. I slowed my car down as I approached, because I was sure that it was a deer and I didn't want it to run in front of my car. I also did not have my headlights on. There was enough daylight to see the deer there without them. I slowly came to a stop right where the mother deer stood with her fawn at her side! She knew my car was approaching her, and yet she did not turn and run away. I was amazed! She was right there at the edge of the road as if she was waiting for me there! I know I looked at her and the fawn standing there looking at me, for at least a couple of minutes! Then she slowly turned around with her fawn at her side, and slowly walked away! She didn't run at all! I just knew in my heart at that moment, that it was a sign from God. Such a feeling of peace came over me at the time. I truly felt that God was showing me that my son was up in heaven at my mother's side! It gave me such strength and an assurance that day, that God was caring for me and that everything was going to be okay.

I know that being strong and carrying on with my life isn't going to be an easy task. It is hard sometimes, to hide my true feelings, but then again, I really shouldn't. People that care about me will always ask me how I am doing, and that's okay. It is much easier to simply say that I am fine, rather than really admit what my heart is feeling—especially in public. But I have learned that it helps sometimes just to say that I have good days and I also have bad days. I have learned that I can't just get through it or just get over it, as some people would want me to do.

The death of my child is something that I will never get over. Someone told me a while ago, to always keep Kyle's memory alive, and that is what I have done, and what I will continue to do, every day of my life. Even though there is never a day that goes by when I haven't cried my eyes out, or wanted to cry, but had to hold it in, I try to struggle through. There also is never a day when I haven't thought of him or mentioned him to someone in passing conversation. Some people think that it is better not to mention my grief and sadness to me, but it actually hurts me more, when someone that is a friend of mine, forgets that part of my life, as if it had never happened. I guess that I treasure it more when Kyle is acknowledged or mentioned to me. He is on my mind and in my thoughts and prayers every day. I can still hear his voice, especially calling his sister's name, or my name, or saying hello to me on the phone. I hope that I will always keep that sound of his voice in my head.

There is always something that I will feel guilty about too. I wish that I would have heeded his words, when he told me not to be sad when he died on the railroad. Instead I tried to stop him from even thinking about dying. Maybe I could have convinced him to quit that dangerous job, and find some other type of work, if only I would have listened to him better. But then I realized that no matter what job he had or where he was, God was calling him home, and there was nothing that I could have done about that. It was Kyle's destiny to go, and it was his time, and he was prepared and happy to go too.

That makes me remember another thought that has kept me going. A loving member of my family once said to me that I should be thank full to God for *lending* me my son for the time that I had him. Kyle was God's child before he was mine. I can't imagine how empty I would have felt if I had never had Kyle at all. I am also thankful to God for *lending* me my daughter Katerina. I must be thankful for the gifts that God has given me, rather than resent Him for what I have lost. Now I know that every moment that I spend with my daughter should be very precious to me. I have to give her all the love that I can, because I know neither of us are ever promised tomorrow.

Because of Kyle's death, I have made sure to tell everyone in my family, and those that I am close to, that I love them unconditionally.

Life is precious, and I will never know if that moment might be the last time that I have to tell someone how much I love them.

I have learned that it is important to settle all differences that I might have had with a friend or with a relative because of this. I know that I should never hold a grudge with someone or stop talking to someone over an argument I might have had with them. It is much better to make up and love them and be kind to them instead. That may be the last chance that I have to make amends.

Kyle's death has taught me that every day should be a holiday. Every day should be the Fourth of July. It may be the last day that I have on this earth, and God wants us all to live with zest and be happy in life. I know now that Kyle had the right idea with his life. He knew that material things didn't matter. He knew that having a lot of money was not what was important. Having friends and helping others was the most important thing to Kyle. He gave all that he had to his friends or to someone that needed it more than he did. That is why he had trouble with his finances. He gave most of his money away. He always had on a smile, and was always ready to cheer someone up if they were down. I know that I need to follow his example. He celebrated life every day. He lived for the moment and he made everyone around him feel that way too. It has reminded me of the handwritten quote by Charles Dickens that he left in his truck. At the time that he died, I felt that the quote was dark and depressing, but now I can see just what Kyle understood and felt from it. Happiness in life is the important thing, and happiness is not achieved through money or material possessions. Happiness is the gift that should be shared with others, and in turn, giving to others and sharing in what you have, fulfills your life. I have learned all these things from Kyle's life and from his death. If not, then his death would have been in vain.

I have also learned that I must go out of my way to help others or talk to people who are lonely. I remember how much Kyle enjoyed talking and visiting with the older generation. His cheerful attitude and friendly smile brought happiness to those who felt empty and depressed. It helped to brighten their day in a way that was much more important than money or gifts.

I have also learned about death and dying gracefully from my Aunt Josephine. She lingered in a nursing home, on only ice chips and a feeding tube for eight months before she died on Christmas Day. She had a lot of faith in God and He gave her the strength to prepare for her death like no one I have ever seen before. While we thought that we were going to visit her and cheer her up, she was spreading happiness and cheer to us instead! Even though she was in great pain from the cancer within her, she would never let us know how she hurt. She delighted in our visits and shared her happiness with us instead. I also think that because our whole family was worrying and praying for Aunt Josephine, our minds were distracted from the sorrow and pa a Christmastime that we felt without Kyle around.

I have learned that I should thank God every day for my life and for my family and my friends and neighbors. I should especially thank God for my daughter Katerina. I have also learned to thank God for the little things in my life. I thank God when I am driving, and I see the light ahead of me change in enough time for me to stop or drive through it safely. I thank God for the ease I have in finding that close parking space. I thank God for keeping me safe during the night and protecting me from harm. I thank God for my health. I thank God for the gifts that he has given me. I thank God for the comfort of my home and for the companionship of my two dogs. I thank God for His love and I thank God for being patient with me in finding Him and loving Him again. I thank God for giving me Kyle and for what I have learned from his life and his death. But most of all, I thank God for my faith.

This book has been a way of preserving that bond between Kyle and me. As his mother, it has been a journey from unquenchable pain toward emotional and physical healing. Through the memories that I have held within me, I can and will keep his precious love alive. It has also been a way of coping with my grief, and a way of growing stronger through my communication with God. From denial, anger, bargaining, depression, and finally acceptance, I have grown stronger through prayer and closer to the Lord. Through the gifts from the Holy Spirit, I have been given the strength to continue on with my life. This precious love from God has helped me to see and feel that my son is still with me.

By surrendering to God, His love has led me on the path toward physical and emotional healing.

"Now faith is the assurance of things hoped for, the conviction of things not seen. And without faith it is impossible to please Him. For whoever would draw near to God must believe that He exists and that He rewards those who seek Him."

Taken from the St. Joseph Edition of the Standard American Bible Hebrews 11:1, 6

Kyle Joseph
8/18/1980–5/13/2005

About the Author

Ms. Petruso lives in a small town in Michigan and enjoys writing, cooking and gardening, as well as music and art. She spends her leisure time playing catch with her two black Labrador retrievers, or working a difficult puzzle. By writing this story about Kyle, from his birth through his death, she has learned to cope with her grief and loss. She hopes that by telling this true story of her son, she will be able to give hope, and spiritual support, to other parents out there who have lost a child. This is her story of how she and her family have survived tragedy and continued on with their lives through prayer and spiritual strength, and blessings from God.